Build your first website with Dja

Go from zero knowledge to your own website using the easiest to learn language on the Internet

Nigel George

Build your first website with Django 2.1

Published by GNW Independent Publishing, Hamilton NSW, Australia

ISBN: 978-0-9946168-6-9 (PRINT)

22 21 20 19 18   2 3 4 5 6 7 8 9

5 x Your Learning with the Django Beginner's Course!

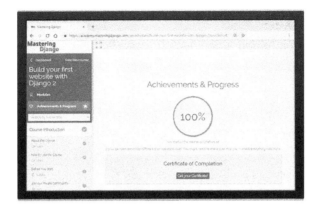

Introducing *Build your first website with Django 2*, a 12-hour on-line course based on the book that will transform you from a complete newbie, to writing and deploying your own website.

You'll be experiencing practical and engaging on-line learning while you **create your own website with the latest version of Django 2**.

Course Bonuses

- ▶ **Over 3 hours of HD video lessons**
- ▶ **Printable transcripts**
- ▶ **Downloadable source code**
- ▶ **Lifetime access to a private Facebook group**
- ▶ **Verified completion certificate to give to potential employers or clients**

Save $50

Go to djbook.io/bookbonus and enter the code **BB50** when you get to the checkout to **save $50 off the full course.**

Results Guaranteed!

Table of Contents

Chapter 4 — Installing Python and Django   33

Chapter 5 — Python Basics   47

Chapter 6 — Your First Django Application   81

Chapter 7 — Creating the Page Model   95

Chapter 8 — Django Templates   109

1

Introduction

Welcome to *Build your first website with Django 2.1:* the second edition of *Build your first website with Python and Django*.

One of the things I love most about the Django community is the great feedback and advice I get from its members. This book, like all my books and courses, is a response to that feedback.

The first edition of this book was released in November 2017. The reason why I am back here less than a year later, is that Django 2.0 was released in December 2017. Since then, the message from the Django community has been loud and clear—you all love Django 2!

Build Your First Website with Django 2.1 remains an introduction to web programming using Django. The primary change between the first and second editions is that the code has been updated to Django 2.1.

The book has proven to be a popular resource with beginners over the last 9 months, however, there is always room for improvement. Based on feedback from the community, I have expanded on some of the concepts presented in the book and clarified a few sections that create confusion.

This book will teach you step by step, and in easy to understand language, how to design, build and deploy a complete website.

The goal of this book is to answer the three most common questions I get from new Django programmers:

1. Why should I use Django—what problems does it help me solve?
2. What if I don't know Python?
3. Forget snippets!—How do I use Django to build a real website?

Ultimately, it's up to you as the reader to judge whether I meet my goals. As always, my commitment remains—write the very best book I can and keep it up to date, so it meets your needs now and in the future.

Who This Book is For

This book is mostly for beginners with no experience with Python, Django or web programming. It's also valuable for experienced programmers who want to learn Django while building a website. Just keep in mind, if you are an experienced programmer, that some parts of the book go deeper into the basics, so feel free to skim to the meatier sections.

A basic understanding of how to write and structure computer programs is an advantage, however, writing well-structured code is something that you pick up naturally the more code you write.

A basic understanding of HTML is also an advantage, but not necessary.

In the few sections that touch on concepts outside of the scope of the book, I provide full references.

Please note that this book is an introduction to Python and Django. While the result of your efforts will be a fully functioning website, there is a great deal more to Django's capabilities than is possible to cover in a single book.

Resources on where to go after you have completed the material in the book are provided in the final chapter—*Next Steps*.

Structure of the Book

This is a project-driven book, rather than dry theory and code snippets.

You will learn by doing—at each step you will put what you have learned into practice so that by the end of the book you will have a functioning website to call your own.

To support your learning, the first four chapters are aimed at answering the first two of the common beginner questions. Namely:

▶ In **Chapter 2**, I outline the benefits of using Django for your websites;

▶ In **Chapter 3**, I provide the high-level outline of the structure of Django and how each of the pieces fit together to create a powerful, scalable website;

▶ In **Chapter 4**, we will install Python and Django; and

▶ In **Chapter 5**, I will give you an introductory tutorial in Python, aimed at covering the elements of Python relevant to Django.

The rest of the book focuses on teaching you Django while you build your website. Each chapter introduces a new aspect of Django, with full source code and a line-by-line explanation of the code, so you know what is going on with your program. I also introduce troubleshooting and debugging as you go so you know what to do when things go wrong.

Software Versions

This is an introductory text that does not require any special functions or libraries, so the latest versions of Python 3 and Django 2.1 are OK. At the time of writing this is Python 3.7.0 and Django 2.1.

All the code in this book will run on Windows, macOS or Linux. While the installation instructions are aimed at Windows users, the fundamentals remain the same—all three have some form of terminal or command window and installation steps are the same on all three platforms.

Coding style is also identical across platforms with one exception—Windows style backslashes are used in file paths. This is to assist Windows users differentiate between Windows' native use of backslashes and Django's implementation of forward slashes in path names. Linux and macOS users, simple need to substitute forward slashes in these cases.

Python 2 or 3?

Unfortunately, this question comes up too often. The simple and *only* answer for beginners is Python 3.

Since the release of version 2.0, Django only supports Python 3.

If you ever have to use Python 2—due to old code or needing a legacy library—the differences between the two versions of Python are not enough to lose sleep over.

Happy Python 3 programmers are happy Python 2 programmers.

Moving on.

Source Code

Source code for the book can be downloaded from `https://djangobook.com/mfdw-source`.

If you can't download the code for any reason, send me an email to `nigel@masteringdjango.com`.

2

Why Django?

Django is one of many web frameworks available, however, over the last decade Django has distinguished itself as a leading framework for developing scalable, secure and maintainable web applications.

This is no fluke.

Django is not the outcome of an academic exercise, or the brainchild of a developer who thought they could do things better.

Django was created in a newsroom environment where "today" is much more important than "clever".

Although how Django simplifies many complex tasks could be considered extremely clever, Django's primary focus on getting stuff done is baked into its DNA.

So, Why Django?

Programming, like most creative pursuits, has many dedicated people who wear their passions on the outside.

It's for this reason that I am very wary of This Software *vs*. That Software comparisons. Bottom line: all programming languages, and the tools and frameworks built on them, have good points and bad points.

It's my firm belief that the only comparison worth considering is pragmatism *vs.* perfection.

Or to put it another way, do you want stable, maintainable code that you can deliver to a deadline? Or do you want a box of arcane magic and boilerplate that will simultaneously make college professors love you and maintainers hate you?

Django has its rough edges, but its pragmatic approach to getting stuff done is where it really stands out from the crowd. Django has plenty of supporters, and a few detractors, so feel free to come to your own conclusions. However, if you want my humble opinion, these are Django's Top 10:

1. Python
2. Batteries included
3. Doesn't get in your way
4. Built-in admin
5. Scalable
6. Battle tested
7. Packages, packages and more packages!
8. Actively developed
9. Stable releases
10. First class documentation

Python

Python is arguably the easiest programming language to learn.

With its use of natural language constructs (e.g., paragraph-like layout and indentation) and simple to learn syntax, Python makes understanding program structure and flow significantly easier to learn than other popular languages.

This is evident in the fact that many introductory programming courses in universities and colleges now use Python as the language of choice.

Python is versatile. It runs websites and is used in many popular desktop applications on PCs and Macs. It can also be found in mobile applications and embedded in many devices. Python is also a popular scripting language for other applications. It's certain that learning Python will benefit you no matter where your career takes you.

Python is popular. Google, one of the world's biggest businesses, uses Python in many of its applications. It's also widely used by professional programmers.

Some interesting facts from the 2017 Stack Overflow Developer Survey[1]:

▶ Python is second only to node.js in growth over the last five years. PHP, Java and Ruby have all declined in popularity.

▶ Python is now more common than PHP.

▶ Python is the most wanted language among all developers, jumping four places since 2016 and beating JavaScript for first place.

▶ Python jobs pay better than traditional Microsoft jobs (C#, C++, VBA and .NET).

Batteries Included

Django inherits its "batteries included" philosophy from Python.

This is often interpreted as meaning that Django includes a lot of extra stuff you don't need. This is not correct. A better analogy is instead of having to open up the language to insert your own power (batteries), you just "flick the switch" and Django does the rest.

---

1   https://stackoverflow.com/insights/survey/2017

In practical terms this means that Django implements some common but complex processes by providing simple tools and wrappers to hide the complexity without compromising power.

Django's batteries are located in the *contrib packages*. The contrib packages are:

▶ **admin**. The Django administration application

▶ **auth**. Django's authentication framework

▶ **contenttypes**. A framework for hooking into Django models

▶ **flatpages**. A framework for managing special case pages like site policies and terms and conditions of use

▶ **gis**. Adds geospatial capabilities to Django

▶ **humanize**. Adds template filters to improve readability of data

▶ **messages**. A framework for managing session- and cookie-based messages

▶ **postgres**. PostgreSQL database specific features

▶ **redirects**. Manages redirects

▶ **sites**. Allows you to operate multiple websites from the one installation

▶ **sitemaps**. Implements sitemap XML files

▶ **staticfiles**. Collects static files from within your apps

▶ **syndication**. A framework for generating syndication feeds

The contrib packages can get a bit complex, so we will only be touching on one or two of them in this book, but as you can see, Django provides a solid list of powerful modules built-in so you don't have to create them yourself.

Doesn't Get in Your Way

When you create a Django application, Django adds no boilerplate, cruft or unnecessary functions. There are no mandatory imports, no required third-party libraries and no XML configuration files.

This can be a bit terrifying when you first create a Django project, as Django's automatic tools (`startproject` and `startapp`) only create a basic settings file, a few folders and some almost empty starter files.

While this might appear to be a bad thing, it's actually a great benefit as Django has provided you with a solid foundation that you can build upon in any way you like.

The result is greater confidence in your code as you know that whatever is in your application you put there.

Built-in Admin

Out of the box, Django provides you with an administration interface for working with your models and managing users, user permissions and groups.

The model interface immediately replaces the need for a separate database administration program for most database functions.

With very simple changes to your admin configuration, you can organize your model fields, show and hide fields, sort, filter and arrange your data to maximize efficiency.

The admin also has an optional model documentation feature that provides automatic documentation for your models.

User management is always important in a modern website and Django provides all that you would expect to add and modify users, change passwords, create user groups, assign permissions and communicate with users.

Like the rest of Django, the admin is also customizable and extendable.

For example, admin display templates can be overridden, and new functionality added for tasks like exporting your model data to a comma-delimited (CSV) file.

Scalable

Django is based on the Model-View-Controller (MVC) design pattern. This means that database, program code (back end) and display code (front end) are separate.

Django takes this one step further by separating code from the static media—images, files, CSS and JavaScript—that make up your site.

These design philosophies allow you to:

▸ Run separate servers for your database, applications and media;

▸ Easily have your media served from a Content Delivery Network (CDN);

▸ Cache content at multiple levels and scopes; and

▸ For really big sites, employ clustering and load-balancing to distribute your website across multiple servers.

Django supports a range of popular third-party vendors for web servers, performance management, caching, clustering and balancing.

It also supports major email and messaging applications and services like OAuth and REST.

Battle Tested

A good way to tell if a web framework is both robust and reliable is to find out how long it has been around, if it's growing and what high-profile sites are using it.

Django was first open-sourced in 2005, after running for several years in the high-demand environment of a news organization.

After over 13 years of growth, Django now not only runs news publishing companies like the Washington Post, but is also running all or part of major global enterprises like Instagram, Disqus, Bitbucket, EventBrite and Zapier.

Django continues to grow in popularity. Djangosites[2] lists over 5200 sites using Django, and that is only for sites that register with Djangosites.

It would be impossible to guess how many pages Django serves every day compared to other technologies, but that is largely irrelevant—Django has proven itself over the years by running some of the most heavily trafficked sites on the Internet. Django continues to grow its user-base today.

Packages, Packages and More Packages!

Just about anything you are likely to do with Django has been done before.

Many of Django's large international community of developers give back to the community by releasing their projects as open-source packages.

The largest repository of these projects can be found on the Django Packages site[3]. At the time of writing, Django Packages lists over 5300 reusable Django apps, sites and tools to use in your own Django projects.

---

2   https://www.djangosites.org/
3   https://djangopackages.org/

A quick tour of popular packages includes:

- **Wagtail**, **Mezzanine** and **django CMS**. Content management systems built on Django.
- **Cookiecutter**. Quick and easy setup of Django project and app structures for more advanced applications
- **Django REST Framework**. Implements a REST API in Django
- **Django allauth**. Facebook, GitHub, Google and Twitter authentication for your Django apps
- **Debug toolbar**. Display debug information as your project is running
- **Django Celery**. Provides Celery integration for Django
- **Oscar**, **Django Shop** and **Cartridge**. E-commerce frameworks for Django (Cartridge is an extension for Mezzanine CMS)

With thousands more packages just like these, it's highly likely that you will find a package that works out of the box, or can be modified to suit your needs, without having to reinvent the wheel.

Actively Developed

One of the biggest risks of open-source is whether there is sufficient interest in the project for it to attract developer support in the long term.

There is no such risk with Django—not only is the project over 13 years old, but it has a long history of consistent releases and it continues to be supported by an active community and a large core team of voluntary contributors who maintain and improve the code base every day.

Django had its first production release in 2008 (version 1.0) and has had three Long Term Support (LTS) releases—1.4, 1.8 and 1.11. The 1.11 LTS release has full support out to the middle of 2020. Django 2.0 was released in December 2017 and the next LTS version, Django 2.2, which is due out in April 2019, will be supported until at least mid-2022.

The Django development team maintains a development roadmap on the Django Project website[4], and have a solid track record of meeting roadmap milestones.

The Django Project is also supported by an independent foundation—the Django Software Foundation—that is a registered non-profit in the US.

Stable Releases

Open-source software projects are, in many cases, more actively developed and more secure than competing proprietary software.

The downside of the ever-evolving development of an open-source software project is the lack of a stable codebase on which to base commercial development.

Django addresses this issue with Long Term Support (LTS) versions of the software and a defined release process.

LTS versions are released with a guaranteed (typically three years) support period. In this period the codebase is guaranteed to remain stable; with patches for bugs, security and data loss 100% compatible with the feature release.

Django's release process ensures that official releases are as stable as possible. After a development phase, each release enters an Alpha phase where a feature freeze is applied.

The new release then moves through Beta and Release Candidate (RC) stages where bugs are worked out of the release. If no major bugs are found for a period after the release candidate, the final will be released (feature release).

After the final has been released, only bug-fixes and security patches are applied. These patches, like the LTS versions, are 100% compatible with the feature release.

First Class Documentation

Even in the very early releases, Django's developers made sure that the documentation was comprehensive and that tutorials were easy to follow.

For me, the documentation should be number one on this list because it was the quality of the documentation that made me choose Django over other options.

This was in 2007 when Django was still version 0.96, before it had made its first official release. The official documentation has only got better in the intervening years.

Django has strong support from community members who produce paid and free learning materials, books, courses and lots of tips, tricks and assistance on their websites.

I am in this latter group—but there are plenty of others. Some of my favorites are Tango With Django[5], anything from Danny and Audrey at TwoScoops Press[6] and the Django Girls[7].

Chapter Summary

In this chapter, we have considered the reasons why you would use Django to develop websites for yourself and your clients.

Django is not the only web framework available, but there are some very strong reasons why it's one of the most popular.

---

[5]   http://www.tangowithdjango.com/
[6]   https://www.twoscoopspress.com/
[7]   https://djangogirls.org/

With a strong design philosophy, robust scalability, security and huge community support, Django now runs some of the most recognized, high traffic enterprises on the Internet.

With a large core team supporting it, Django will continue to grow in the future.

In the next chapter we will explore the mechanics of how Django works. We will do this from a high level, avoiding digging into code right away, so you can gain an understanding of how all the different pieces fit together to make your Django website work.

3

Django Overview

In this chapter, we will cover the basic structure of Django and how all the pieces come together to create a web application.

After researching the Internet and analyzing feedback from my own audience, I believe most queries from those considering learning Django come down to two common questions:

1. Why should I use Django—What problems can Django solve?; and
2. How does it all fit together?

The first chapter explained *what* Django does and *why* it was created. In this chapter we will look at *how* Django works. We will discuss big picture concepts; there is almost no code in this chapter. This is entirely deliberate.

Django is a large, complex project that can be difficult to grasp piecemeal. Taking the time to understand at a high level how those many parts come together makes the journey to becoming a competent Django programmer much easier.

Those of you keen to start coding should feel free to jump ahead to the next chapter, but you will almost certainly come back here to gain a full understanding of Django. It's best to be patient and make sure you absorb the material in this chapter before you move on.

The Big Picture—How Django is Structured

Django is a *Model-View-Controller* (MVC) framework. MVC is a software design pattern that aims to separate a software application into three interconnected parts:

1. The **model** provides the interface with the database containing the application data;
2. The **view** decides what information to present to the user and collects information from the user; and
3. The **controller** manages the business logic for the application and acts as an information broker between the model and the view.

Django uses slightly different terminology in its implementation of MVC (Figure 3-1). In Django:

1. The **model** is functionally the same. Django's Object-Relational Mapping (ORM—more on the ORM later) provides the interface to the application database;
2. The **template** provides display logic and is the interface between the user and your Django application; and
3. The **view** manages the bulk of the applications data processing, application logic and messaging.

The MVC design pattern has been used for both desktop and web applications for many years, so there are variations on this theme—of which Django is no exception. If you wish to dig a bit deeper into the MVC design pattern, be warned that people can be quite passionate about what is a different interpretation of the same thing. To borrow a quote from the Django development team:

> *At the end of the day, of course, it comes down to getting stuff done. And, regardless of how things are named, Django gets stuff done in a way that's most logical to us.*

I whole-heartedly agree.

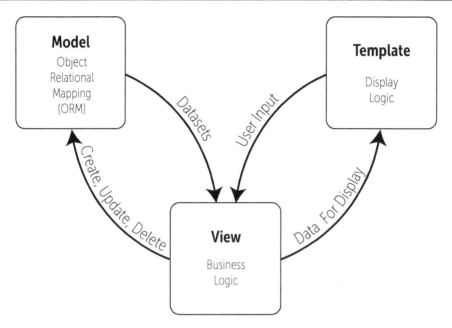

Figure 3-1. *A pictorial description of the Model–Template–View (MTV) pattern, Django's implementation of the MVC design pattern.*

Django Models

Django's models provide an Object-relational Mapping (ORM) to the underlying database. ORM is a powerful programming technique that makes working with data and relational databases much easier.

Most common databases are programmed with some form of Structured Query Language (SQL), however each database implements SQL in its own way. SQL can be quite complex and difficult to learn. An ORM tool, on the other hand, provides a simple mapping between an *object* (the 'O' in ORM) and the underlying database. This means that the programmer doesn't need to know the database structure, nor does it require complex SQL to manipulate and retrieve data (Figure 3-2).

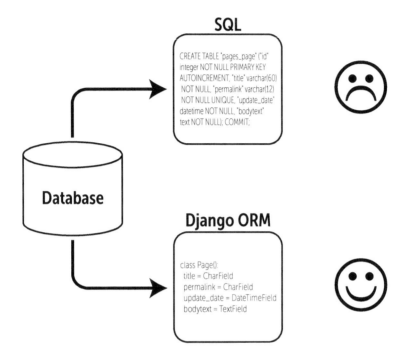

Figure 3-2. An ORM allows for simple manipulation of data without having to write complex SQL.

In Django, the model is the object that is mapped to the database. When you create a model, Django creates a corresponding table in the database (Figure 3-3), without you having to write a single line of SQL. Django prefixes the table name with the name of your Django application (more on Django applications later).

The model also links related information in the database. In Figure 3-4, a second model is created to keep track of the courses a user is enrolled in. Repeating all the user's information in the yourapp_Course table would be against good design principles, so we instead create a *relationship* (the 'R' in ORM) between the yourapp_Course table and the yourapp_UserProfile table.

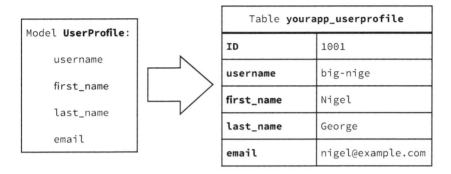

Figure 3-3. *Creating a Django model creates a corresponding table in the database.*

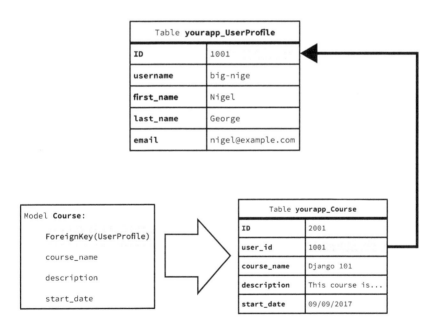

Figure 3-4. *Relationships between tables are created by foreign key links in Django models.*

This relationship is created by linking the models with a *foreign key*—in other words the user_id field in the yourapp_Course table is a key field that is linked to the id field in the foreign table yourapp_UserProfile.

This is a simplification—for example, Django doesn't link foreign keys directly, but uses an intermediate table—but is a handy overview of how Django's ORM uses the model data to create database tables. We will be revisiting models a few times throughout the book, so don't worry if you don't 100% understand what is going on right now. Things become clearer once you have had the chance to build real models.

Supported Databases

Django officially supports four databases:

▶ PostgreSQL
▶ MySQL
▶ SQLite
▶ Oracle

There are also several third-party applications available if you need to connect to an unofficially supported database.

The preference for most Django developers, myself included, is PostgreSQL. MySQL is also a common database backend for Django. Installing and configuring a database is not a task for a beginner. Luckily, Django installs and configures SQLite automatically, with no input from you, so we will be using SQLite throughout this book.

I cover deploying to a MySQL database in Chapter 14. If you do wish to work with another production database like PostgreSQL, you can find more advanced information on the Django Book website[1].

---

1   https://djangobook.com

Which Database is Better?

Easy one first—SQLite is for early development and testing. It should not be used in production. Ever.

Next easiest answer—Oracle is for big corporations with deep pockets. You are unlikely to need to decide whether to use Oracle unless you join a big enterprise, and then you might find it's your *only* choice.

As for PostgreSQL and MySQL—There are definite reasons why PostgreSQL is a better database than MySQL. However, by the time you have learned enough programming to understand why, you will be able to judge for yourself. Most often the choice will have been made for you by the client, your employer or the web host.

Smart programmers avoid this kind of argument—use PostgreSQL if you can, otherwise MySQL is fine too.

Django Templates

A Django template is a text file designed to separate an application's data from the way it is presented. Django's templates are not limited to HTML—they can be used for rendering several text formats. If you want to explore these more advanced uses for Django templates, check out my other book—*Mastering Django: Core*[2].

The design of Django's templates is based on several core principles, however three are key:

1. A template system should separate program logic from design;
2. Templates should discourage redundancy—Don't Repeat Yourself (DRY); and
3. The template system should be safe and secure—code execution in the template must be forbidden.

---

2   https://djangobook.com/mastering-django-core/

Separate Logic From Design

Web design and web programming are two very different disciplines. For all but the smallest projects, design and programming are not done by the same people; in many cases not even the same company.

When Django's creators first considered the design of Django's template system, it was clear that programmers and website designers must be able to work independently of each other. The result is the Django template language (DTL)—a plain-text scripting language that uses *tags* to provide presentation logic for deciding what content to display in the template. This is easier to understand with a simple example:

```
<h1>Your Order Information</h1>
<p>Dear {{ person_name }},</p>
```

This could be the first couple of lines of an order confirmation page, displayed on a website after the user has made a purchase. You will notice that most of this code is plain HTML. The small bit of script in bold is a Django *variable tag*. When this template is rendered in your browser, the template will replace the variable {{ person_name }} with the name passed to the template by the view.

As this is plain-text and HTML, a designer does not need to know anything about Django to be able to create a Django template. All the designer has to do is add a placeholder (e.g. HTML comment tag) for the programmer to replace with a Django tag when coding the website.

The other major advantage of this approach is that the bulk of the template is plain HTML. A programmer can create a good-looking website without a designer by downloading an HTML template from the Internet and adding Django template tags. This also works with Bootstrap templates and site templates heavy in JavaScript.

Don't Repeat Yourself (DRY)

DRY is a term that comes up often in Django discussions as it's one of Django's core principles. The DRY principle is particularly evident in how Django uses *template inheritance*. To better understand how template inheritance helps minimize repetition and redundant code, let's first examine a typical webpage layout (Figure 3-5).

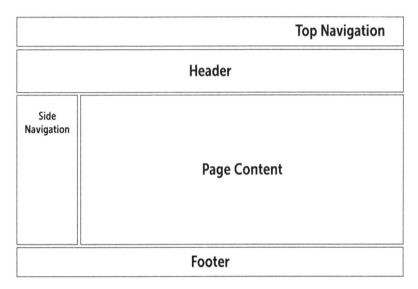

Figure 3-5. A typical webpage layout with common elements such as a header, footer and navigation.

This page layout has top navigation, a header image, left side navigation, the main content of the page and a footer. If you only wanted to create a few webpages, you could get away with copying the front page and simply changing the content and saving each different page as an HTML file.

The problem is, not only are we repeating a lot of code, but maintaining a large site could quickly get out of hand—what if you needed to change the template? You would have to make the change on every single page in your site!

We fix this problem by creating a parent template that contains content common to the entire website, and then creating child templates that inherit these common features, adding any content unique to the child template (Figure 3-6).

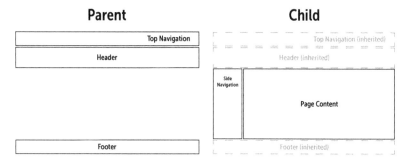

Figure 3-6. *A child template only adds structure and content unique to the child. All common elements are inherited from the parent template.*

You will notice I included the sidebar navigation in the child here. It's common for certain pages on a site to have limited navigation, so not every page will need the side navigation.

Django supports multiple inheritance too so, following on from the above example, you could have a child template that adds only the side navigation to the parent and then have a third template that inherits from the child and adds the content.

The only limit to how you slice and dice Django's template inheritance is practicality—if you have templates inheriting more than one or two deep, you should re-evaluate your site design.

Django's templates—including how to create your own parent and child templates for your website project—are covered in Chapter 8.

Template Security

Django's philosophy is that the Internet is insecure enough, without introducing security issues by allowing Python code execution within webpage templates. Django's solution to template security vulnerabilities is simple—code execution is forbidden.

The DTL provides display logic only, this includes:

▶ Displaying variables—this can be simple text like a user's name, or more complex data like HTML formatted text.

▶ Choosing which content to display based on logical checks. E.g., if a user is logged in, then display user menu or user-only content.

▶ Iterating over lists of data—most often used to insert database information into HTML lists.

▶ Formatting data—for example, date formatting, text manipulation and other filters that act on the data.

Things you can't do in a Django template:

▶ Execute Python code

▶ Assign a value to a variable

▶ Perform advanced logic

Django's templates also add additional security features like automatically escaping all strings, *Cross-Site Scripting* protection and *Cross-Site Request Forgery* protection. These last two are more advanced topics outside the scope of a beginner's book, but it's helpful to understand that Django's templates are secure by default, so you don't have to worry about accidentally introducing security issues into your website.

These restrictions only apply to the Django template language. There are no restrictions on you adding your own JavaScript, for example, to Django templates.

Django Views

Django's views are the information brokers of a Django application. A view sources data from your database (or an external data source or service) and delivers it to a template. For a web application the view delivers webpage content and templates, for a RESTful API this content could be properly formatted JSON data.

The view makes decisions on what data gets delivered to the template—either by acting on input from the user, or in response to other business logic and internal processes.

Each Django view performs a specific function and has an associated template. Views are represented by either a Python function, or a method of a Python class. In the early days of Django, there were only function-based views, however, as Django has grown over the years, Django's developers added class-based views.

Class-based views add extensibility to Django's views, as well as built-in views that make creating common views (like displaying a list of articles) easier to implement. Don't worry too much about the differences between function- and class-based views now, we will be covering both in more detail later in the book.

To ease the burden on programmers, many common display tasks have built-in views in Django. There are four built-in function-based views for displaying error pages:

▶ The 404 (page not found) view

▶ The 500 (server error) view

▶ The 403 (HTTP forbidden) view

▶ The 400 (bad request) view

There are also several class-based views for simplifying common display tasks. They include:

▶ `ListView` for displaying a list of data objects (e.g. list all articles)

▶ `DetailView` for displaying a single object (e.g. individual article)

▶ `RedirectView` for redirecting to another URL

▶ `FormView` for displaying a form

Additional class-based generic date views for showing day, week, month and yearly collections of objects like blog posts and articles are also provided by Django.

URLconf—Tying it all Together

Our website is not much use if we can't navigate around it—we need to tell the view what to display in the browser based on what the user has requested.

Navigation in a Django website is the same as any other website—pages and other content are accessed via a Uniform Resource Locator (URL). When a user clicks on a link on a website, a request for that URL is sent to Django (Figure 3-7).

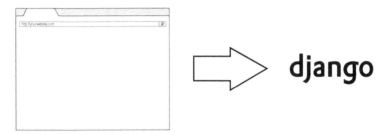

Figure 3-7. *The browser request for your site home page is sent directly to Django.*

Once Django receives the requested URL, it must decide which view will deal with the request. You, as the programmer, decide which view to serve at which URL by creating a URL Configuration (URLconf for short) in a Python file named `urls.py`. When Django finds a URL in `urls.py` that matches the requested URL it calls the view associated with that URL (Figure 3-8).

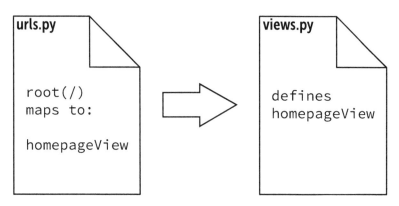

Figure 3-8. *Django maps the requested URL to a view.*

The selected view then renders the content to a template, as per the business logic in the view, and sends the rendered content back to your browser for display (Figure 3-9).

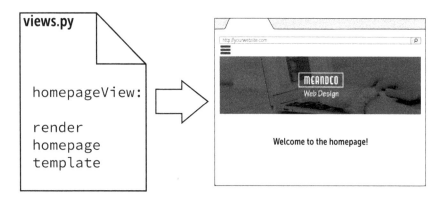

Figure 3-9. *The view tells Django what template to use when sending content back to the browser.*

Of course, this is a simplification—Django can collect much more complex data than a URL from the browser and views don't just render webpages. There is also a whole other layer of Django goodness that sits between the browser request and your view's response, which Django rather cleverly calls *middleware*. Middleware allows you to do tons of cool stuff with your data, but these are advanced topics which we won't cover in this book.

The takeaway here is, regardless of how complex a website gets, this simple process underlies all the communication between Django, the browser and the end user.

Chapter Summary

In this chapter we gained a high-level understanding of the structure of Django and how Django communicates with the browser to display your site content.

We examined some of the key files that are created as a part of your Django application and how they work together to collect information from the user, decide what data needs to be sent back to the browser and how that data is to be displayed.

In Chapter 5 we start programming, but first we need install Python and Django on your computer, which is the subject of the next chapter.

4

Installing Python and Django

Before you can start learning Django, you must install some software on your computer. Fortunately, this is a simple three step process:

1. Install Python;
2. Install a Python Virtual Environment; and
3. Install Django.

If this doesn't sound familiar to you don't worry. In this chapter, I assume you have never installed software from the command line before, so I will lead you through it step by step.

This chapter is written for those of you running Windows. While there is a strong Linux and macOS user base for Django, most new users are on Windows. If you are using Mac or Linux, there are numerous resources on the Internet—the best place to start being Django's own installation instructions[1].

For Windows users, your computer can be running any recent version of Windows (7, 8.1 or 10). This chapter also assumes you're installing Django on a desktop or laptop computer and will be using the development server and SQLite to run all the code in this book. This is by far the easiest and best way to set up Django when you are first starting out.

---

1   https://docs.djangoproject.com/en/2.1/intro/install/

Installing Python

Python is used by a lot of Windows applications so it's possible that it is already installed on your system. You can check this out by opening a command prompt or running PowerShell and typing `python` at the prompt.

If Python isn't installed you'll get a message saying that Windows can't find Python. If Python is installed, the `python` command will open the Python interactive interpreter:

```
C:\Users\Nigel>python
Python 3.6.0 (v3.6.0:41df79263a11, Dec 23 2016, 07:18:10)
[MSC v.1900 32 bit (Intel)] on win32
Type "help", "copyright", "credits" or "license" for more
information.
>>>
```

You can see in the above example that my PC is running Python 3.6.0. Django 2.1 is compatible with Python version 3.5 and later. If you have an older version of Python, you will have to install Python 3.7 for the code in this book to work.

If you have Python 3.5 or 3.6 I still recommend you install Python 3.7 to ensure you have the latest version installed on your machine.

Assuming Python 3 is not installed on your system, you first need to get the installer. Go to `https://www.python.org/downloads/` and click the big yellow button that says "Download Python 3.x.x".

At the time of writing, the latest version of Python is 3.7.0, but it may have been updated by the time you read this, so the numbers may be slightly different.

Once you have downloaded the Python installer, go to your downloads folder and double click the file `python-3.x.x.msi` to run the installer. The installation process is the same as any other Windows program, so if you have installed software before, there should be no problem here; however, there is one extremely important customization you **_must_** make.

By default, the Python executable is not added to the Windows PATH. For Django to work properly, Python must be listed in the PATH statement. Fortunately, this is easy to rectify—when the Python installer screen opens, make sure **Add Python 3.7 to PATH** is checked before installing (Figure 4-1).

Do not forget this step!

It will solve most problems that arise from incorrect mapping of pythonpath (an important variable for Python installations) in Windows.

Figure 4-1. *Check the "Add Python 3.7 to PATH" box before installing.*

Once Python is installed, restart Windows and then type python at the command prompt. You should see something like this:

```
PS C:\Users\nigel> python
Python 3.7.0 (v3.7.0:1bf9cc5093, Jun 27 2018, 04:06:47)
[MSC v.1914 32 bit (Intel)] on win32
Type "help", "copyright", "credits" or "license" for more
information.
>>>
```

There is one more important thing to do. Exit out of Python (CTRL-Z then ENTER key), then type the following at the command prompt:

```
python -m pip install -U pip
```

This command will either print a message saying pip is up to date, or give an output similar to this:

```
C:\Users\nigel>python -m pip install -U pip
Collecting pip
  Downloading ...0/pip-18.0-py2.py3-none-any.whl (1.3MB)
    100% |############################| 1.3MB 4.3MB/s
Installing collected packages: pip
  Found existing installation: pip 10.0.1
    Uninstalling pip-10.0.1:
      Successfully uninstalled pip-10.0.1
Successfully installed pip-18.0
```

You don't need to understand exactly what this command does right now; put briefly pip is the Python package manager. It's used to install Python packages—pip is actually a recursive acronym for "Pip Installs Packages". pip is important for the next stage of our install process, but first we need to make sure we are running the latest version of pip (18.0 in this example), which is exactly what this command does.

Installing a Python Virtual Environment

When you are writing new software programs, it's possible (and common!) to modify dependencies and environment variables that your other software depends on. This can cause numerous problems, so should be avoided.

A Python virtual environment solves this problem by wrapping all the dependencies and environment variables that your new software needs into a file system separate from the rest of the software on your computer.

The virtual environment tool in Python is called `virtualenv` and we install it from the command line using `pip`:

```
pip install virtualenv
```

The output from your command window will either say that the requirement is already satisfied (i.e. `virtualenv` is up to date), or print out something like this (your version numbers may be different):

```
C:\Users\nigel>pip install virtualenv
  Collecting virtualenv
  Downloading virtualenv-16.0.0-py2.py3-none-any.whl
(1.8MB)
    100% |############################| 1.8MB 323kB/s
Installing collected packages: virtualenv
Successfully installed virtualenv-16.0.0
```

Creating a Project Directory

Before we create our Django project, we first need to create a project folder. The project folder can go anywhere on your computer, although it's highly recommended that it be created somewhere in your user directory, so you don't get permission issues later on. A good place for your project in Windows is your My Documents folder.

Create a new folder on your system. I have named the folder `mfdw_project`, but you can give the folder any name that makes sense to you.

For the next step you need to be in a command window (terminal on Linux and macOS). The easiest way to do this on Windows is to open

Windows Explorer, hold the SHIFT key and right-click the folder to get the context menu and click on **Open command window here** (Figure 4-2).

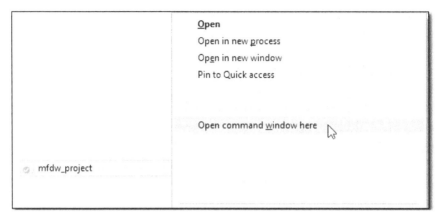

Figure 4-2. Hold the shift key and right-click a folder to open a command window.

Terminal in Windows 10

If you are running newer versions of Windows 10, the command prompt has been replaced by PowerShell. For the examples in this book, the command prompt and PowerShell are functionally the same and all commands will run in PowerShell unmodified.

Once you have created your project folder, you need to create a virtual environment for your project by typing `virtualenv env_mfdw` at the command prompt you just opened:

```
C:\Users\...\mfdw_project>virtualenv env_mfdw
```

Again, the name of the virtual environment is not important; you can change the name to suit your project. On my system the output from this command looks like this:

```
Using base prefix 'c:\\users\\nigel\\appdata\\local\\
programs\\python\\python37-32'
New python executable in D:\OneDrive\Documents\mfdw_
project\env_mfdw\Scripts\python.exe
Installing setuptools, pip, wheel...done.
```

Once virtualenv has finished setting up your new virtual environment, open Windows Explorer and have a look at what virtualenv created for you. In your project directory you will now see a folder called \env_mfdw (or whatever name you gave the virtual environment). If you open the folder you will see the following:

```
\Include
\Lib
\Scripts
\tcl
pip-selfcheck.json
```

If you look inside the \Lib folder, you will see virtualenv has created a complete Python installation for you, separate from your other software, so you can work on your project without affecting any of the other software on your system.

To use this new Python virtual environment we have to activate it, so let's go back to the command prompt and type the following:

```
env_mfdw\scripts\activate
```

This will run the activate script inside your virtual environment's \scripts folder. You will notice your command prompt has now changed:

```
(env_mfdw) C:\Users\...\mfdw_project>
```

The env_mfdw at the beginning of the command prompt lets you know that you are running in the virtual environment. Our next step is to install Django.

Oops! Script Error!

If you are using PowerShell and running this script for the first time, the `activate` command will throw a permission error.

If this happens to you, open PowerShell as an administrator and run the command:

```
Set-ExecutionPolicy remoteSigned
```

Once you have run this command, the activation script will run.

Installing Django

Now that we have Python installed and are running a virtual environment, installing Django is super easy, just type the command:

```
pip install "django>=2.1,<2.2"
```

This will instruct `pip` to install the latest version of Django 2.1 into your virtual environment. Your command output should look like this:

```
(env_mfdw) ...>pip install "django>=2.1,<2.2"

Collecting django<2.2,>=2.1
  Downloading .../Django-2.1-py3-none-any.whl (7.3MB)
    100% |##############################| 7.3MB 2.9MB/s
Collecting pytz (from django<2.2,>=2.1)
  Downloading .../pytz-2018.5-py2.py3-none-any.whl
Installing collected packages: pytz, django
Successfully installed django-2.1 pytz-2018.5
```

To test whether the installation worked, at your virtual environment command prompt, start the Python interactive interpreter by typing `python` and hitting Enter. If the installation was successful, you should be able to import the module `django`:

```
(env_mfdw) C:\Users\...\mfdw_project>python
Python 3.7.0 (v3.7.0:1bf9cc5093, Jun 27 2018, 04:06:47)
[MSC v.1914 32 bit (Intel)] on win32
Type "help", "copyright", "credits" or "license" for more
information.
>>> import django
>>> django.get_version()
'2.1'
```

Don't forget to exit the Python interpreter when you are done.

Starting a Project

Once you've installed Python and Django, you can take the first step in developing a Django application by creating a Django *project*.

A Django project is a collection of settings and files for a single Django website. To create a new Django project we'll be using a special command to auto-generate the folders, files and code that make up a Django project. This includes a collection of settings for an instance of Django, database configuration, Django-specific options and application-specific settings.

I am assuming at this stage you are still running the virtual environment from the previous installation step. If not, you will have to start it again with env_mfdw\scripts\activate\.

From your virtual environment command line, run the following command:

```
django-admin startproject mfdw_site
```

This command will automatically create a mfdw_site folder in your project folder as well as all the necessary files for a basic, but fully functioning Django website. Feel free to explore what startproject created now if you wish, we will be going into greater detail on what each file does in Chapter 6.

Creating a Database

Django includes several applications by default (e.g., the admin program and user management and authentication). Some of these applications makes use of at least one database table, so we need to create tables in the project database before we can use them. To do this, change into the mfdw_site folder created in the last step (type cd mfdw_site at the command prompt) and run the following command:

```
python manage.py migrate
```

The migrate command creates a new SQLite database and any necessary database tables according to the settings file created by the startproject command (more on the settings file later). If all goes to plan, you'll see a message for each migration it applies:

```
(env_mfdw) ...\mfdw_site>python manage.py migrate
Operations to perform:
  Apply all migrations: admin, auth, contenttypes,
sessions
Running migrations:
  Applying contenttypes.0001_initial... OK
  Applying auth.0001_initial... OK
  Applying admin.0001_initial... OK
  ### several more migrations (not shown)
```

The Development Server

Let's verify your Django project works. Change into the outer mfdw_site directory and run the following command:

```
python manage.py runserver
```

This will start the Django development server—a lightweight Web server written in Python. The development server was created so you can develop things rapidly, without having to deal with configuring a production server until you're ready for deployment.

When the server starts, Django will output a few messages before telling you that the development server is up and running at `http://127.0.0.1:8000/`.

If you were wondering, 127.0.0.1 is the IP address for local host, or your local computer. The 8000 on the end is telling you that Django is listening at port 8000 on your local host.

You can change the port number if you want to, but I have never found a good reason to change it, so best to keep it simple and leave it at the default.

Now that the server is running, visit `http://127.0.0.1:8000/` with your web browser. You'll see Django's default welcome page, complete with a cool animated rocket (Figure 4-3). It worked!

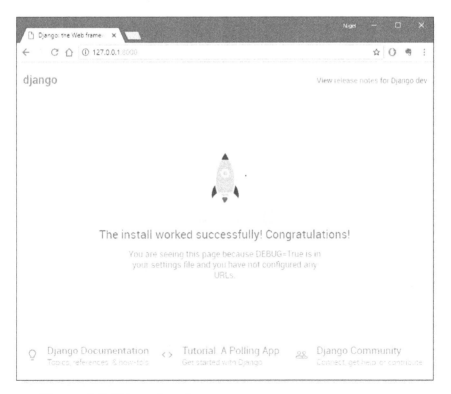

Figure 4-3. Django's welcome page.

TIP: Remember the startup sequence

It will help to make a note of this sequence, so you know how to start your Django project each time you return to the examples in this book:

1. Shift right-click your project folder to open a command window.
2. Type in `env_mfdw\scripts\activate` to run your virtual environment.
3. Change into your site directory (`cd mfdw_site`) to run `manage.py` commands (e.g. `runserver`).

Text Editor

One final note—to do any productive coding, you need to have a text editor installed. Programs like Notepad and common word processing applications are definitely *not* suitable for writing code.

It's up to you what tools you use for software development. Online arguments over the best code editor or IDE are as numerous and as entertaining as arguments over the best programming language.

They're also just as pointless.

Bottom line, there are dozens of different text editors available, most of them either entirely free to download and use, or inexpensive. They all have their pros and cons.

If you don't know much about text editors, I use Microsoft Visual Studio Code. It's free and works great on Windows, Linux and macOS. You can get it from `https://code.visualstudio.com/`.

All the code and examples in this book do not require any particular editor or special tools to run. If you already have a preferred text editor, or someone you trust says you should use editor XYZ, no problem—use what you are comfortable with.

Chapter Summary

In this chapter we installed Python and Django on your computer. In the next chapter, we will start writing some code with a primer on the Python language.

To write code in Django, you need to know a bit about Python first (assuming you have not written any Python code before). The next chapter will give you enough Python programming skills to ensure that when you get to programming Django, you will find writing and understanding the code much easier.

5

Python Basics

In this chapter we are going to be spending a bit of time learning the basics of Python. This chapter is written for beginners who don't have any knowledge of Python or Django. If you have some basic programming knowledge of Python, feel free to skip to the next chapter.

It might seem strange that the first bit of real coding we do in a Django book is in Python, but given that Django is written in Python, it makes perfect sense. If you understand the basics of Python, you will be able to understand Django in a much more comprehensive way. For example, by having a greater understanding of Python, you will be able to identify the bits of Django that are plain Python and the bits that are unique to Django.

The Python Tutorial

This chapter is only meant to be a very basic introduction to Python so you can better understand how Django works. It's not meant to be a complete tutorial on Python, that would require an entire book on its own!

I highly recommend that, to get full benefit out of Django, you should expand your knowledge of Python as soon as possible. The best place to start is the official Python Tutorial[1]

Code Layout—Readability Counts

One of the founding principles behind Python's design is that code is read much more often than it's written. Once a piece of code is written, it often passes through many hands—other developers, documentation authors, auditors and testers. Experienced programmers will also tell you that being able to understand your own code many months, or even years, after you wrote it is extremely important.

Under this guiding principle, Python was designed to mimic natural written English as much as possible. One of these design choices was to use whitespace as a delimiter, rather than braces ({}), or the BEGIN\END type statements used by other languages.

A delimiter is something that defines the beginning or the end of a block of related text. Consider the following:

```
# Kate's Awesome Nachos

1. Collect Ingredients:
    a. Large bag of corn chips
    b. Can of refried beans (preferably chili)
    c. Jar of salsa (not hot!)
    d. Grated cheese
    e. Guacamole
2. Prepare Nachos:
    a. Tip bag of corn chips in oven dish
    b. Spread refried beans over corn chips
    c. Pour on jar of salsa
    d. Top with cheese
3. Cook in oven for 20 mins
4. Serve with guacamole
```

We can easily understand each step of this simple (but delicious!) recipe because it's formatted in a way that all English speakers can understand—relevant information is grouped together in sentences and paragraphs and indentation is used so we can differentiate between Step 1, collecting the ingredients and Step 2, preparation of the nachos.

Python treats whitespace the same way, for example the ingredients written as a Python list may look like:

```
ingredients = [
    "corn chips",
    "refried beans",
    "salsa",
    "grated cheese",
    "guacamole",
]
```

You will notice that Python lists use brackets ([]) as a delimiter, with the indentation and surrounding whitespace clearly differentiating where the list starts and ends. (More on lists shortly.)

Functions for preparing and cooking the nachos might be written like this:

```
def prepare_nachos(ingredients):
    nachos = ""
    for ingredient in ingredients[:4]:
        nachos+=ingredient
    cook_nachos(nachos)

def cook_nachos(nachos):
    # cook in oven for 20mins
```

Now this is a rather silly example, but I bet that you found it easy to follow—even without quite understanding Python syntax. Our list of ingredients is broken up into one ingredient per line to create our ingredients list, and we have used indentation to differentiate between the two Python functions (prepare_nachos and cook_nachos) and the code that belongs to each function.

Here are some real examples that you will see later in the book:

```
# A list from the settings.py file:

INSTALLED_APPS = [
    'pages.apps.PagesConfig',
    'django.contrib.admin',
```

```
        'django.contrib.auth',
        'django.contrib.contenttypes',
        'django.contrib.sessions',
        'django.contrib.messages',
        'django.contrib.staticfiles',
    ]

    # A function from views.py

    def index(request, pagename):
        pagename = '/' + pagename
        pg = Page.objects.get(permalink=pagename)
        context = {
            'title': pg.title,
            'content': pg.bodytext,
            'last_updated': pg.update_date,
            'page_list': Page.objects.all(),
        }
        return render(request, 'pages/page.html', context)
```

I don't expect you to understand this code right now, but as you can see, the layout of the code makes it easy to follow without you necessarily understanding exactly what's going on.

Indentation and intuitive use of whitespace are not the only stylistic conventions designed to make Python code more readable. Python has a complete style guide called **PEP8**[2]. I strongly encourage you to read this document, absorb what it has to say any try to follow **PEP8**'s recommendations in all your programming.

Interactive Interpreter

Python is a *scripted* language. This means that, instead of having to compile your code before it can be run, the Python interpreter runs each line of your code directly.

This allows you to use the Python interpreter interactively, simply by typing python at a command prompt. Try this now. You should get an output something like this:

```
C:\Users\nigel\OneDrive\Documents\mfdw_project> python
Python 3.7.0 (v3.7.0:1bf9cc5093, Jun 27 2018, 04:06:47)
[MSC v.1914 32 bit (Intel)] on win32
Type "help", "copyright", "credits" or "license" for more
information.
>>>
```

Those three greater-than symbols (>>>) is what's called the *primary prompt* and indicates that Python is in interactive mode and ready for you to input commands. Try these exercises by typing each command at the primary prompt and hitting enter:

1. `1+2`
2. `4*5`
3. `14/5`
4. `14//5`
5. `14%5`
6. `x = "Hello"`
7. `y = "There"`
8. `print(x+y)`
9. `print(x,y)`
10. `print(x,y, sep="-")`
11. `csv = "one,two,three"`
12. `lst = csv.split(",")`
13. `lst`

How did you go? This is the output you should have seen in your terminal window:

```
>>> 1+2
3
>>> 4*5
```

```
20
>>> 14/5
2.8
>>> 14//5
2
>>> 14%5
4
>>> x = "Hello"
>>> y = "There"
>>> print(x+y)
HelloThere
>>> print(x,y)
Hello There
>>> print(x,y, sep="-")
Hello-There
>>> csv = "one,two,three"
>>> lst = csv.split(",")
>>> lst
['one', 'two', 'three']
>>>
```

So, let's have a quick look at what we did here.

The first three commands should be easy to follow—you are using Python as a calculator to perform simple addition, multiplication and division. But what about examples 4 and 5?

In example 4 we are performing what is called integer division, so 14//5 is returning the result of 14 divided by 5 without the remainder. And how would you find out the remainder? Use the modulo operator (%)—which is exactly what we are doing in example 5. So 14%5 returns the remainder after dividing 14 by 5.

In examples 6 to 10, things are getting a bit more interesting. In examples 6 and 7, we are simply assigning a string to two new variables. If you have ever used another programming language, you will notice that neither of these variables must be declared before assigning a value to the variable. Python shortcuts this extra cruft by creating a variable when you assign something to it.

You will also notice in examples 6 and 7 I didn't have to declare the new variables as strings. This is because Python is *dynamically typed*, meaning that Python assumes the type of a variable by what you assign to it. In this case, Python assumes that x and y are strings because you assigned strings to them.

Warning—dynamic typing can be dangerous!

The type of a variable is not fixed once assigned so, for example, this is perfectly legal in Python:

```
a=1
a="one"
a=["one"]
```

You can guess why I am putting this fact in a warning box—dynamic typing is powerful and intuitive, but can lead to some interesting errors. It's always a good idea to use variable names that give some indication as to the type (e.g., `user_count` or `names_list`).

Now that we have assigned the strings "Hello" and "There" to variables x and y respectively, we are employing one of Python's most useful functions—`print()`—to print some results out to the terminal. In example 8 we are using the + operator to concatenate—or join—the two strings.

In example 9, we are using the comma (,) to separate x and y; which is basically saying "print x and a space and then print y". The space is the default separator when printing variables. Like most things in Python, this default behavior can be overridden, which is what we are doing in example 10—overriding the space with `sep="-"` and now the variables print out with a dash (-) instead of a space separating them.

The last two examples demonstrate how Python can tackle more complex problems in a simple and intuitive way. The string csv might be a single line from a comma-delimited spreadsheet file that you need to import into

Python. The `string` class in Python has many methods built in to allow you to manipulate strings.

One of those methods is `split()`. `split()` allows you to split a string into a Python list using the string you pass to `split()` as a delimiter. In this case, we are using a comma (`,`) as the delimiter which splits our string "`one,two,three`" at the commas, producing a list of three items (`['one', 'two', 'three']`).

Testing Code With the Interactive Interpreter

The examples so far have been simple, but the takeaway is that anything that runs in Python will run from the interactive interpreter. This is supremely useful for working out how to write code to solve a problem or produce the output you want.

This simple, iterative way that you can work with Python makes the development process much quicker and far less painful that the write-compile-test-rewrite cycle of other programming languages.

You can test code with the interactive interpreter by simply cutting and pasting the code from your editor into the terminal window, or you can type the code in at the primary prompt. It's important to understand, however, how Python interprets more complex code. For example, type this at the primary prompt:

```
for i in range(5):
```

This is the start of a `for` loop (more on `for` loops a bit later). For the sake of this example, I am using the `for` loop to demonstrate what Python does with this command. Notice, when you hit Enter, that Python dropped to the next line and instead of the command prompt (`>>>`), there is now an ellipsis (`...`). This is because Python is waiting for more input from you. The ellipsis is referred to as Python's *secondary prompt*.

This is where most beginners trip up, remember: **whitespace matters**. So if you just start typing at the secondary prompt this is what happens:

```
>>> for i in range(5):
... print(i)
File "<stdin>", line 2
    print(i)
        ^
IndentationError: expected an indented block
>>>
```

The interactive interpreter doesn't automatically indent your code—you must add the indentation yourself. You can do this by either adding four spaces, or hitting the tab key, like so:

```
>>> for i in range(5):
...     print(i)
```

You may need to hit Enter once more to tell Python that you have finished entering code and the loop will run:

```
>>> for i in range(5):
...     print(i)
...
0
1
2
3
4
>>>
```

Very cool. To exit the interactive interpreter, you can either type exit() at the Python prompt or type CTRL-Z on your keyboard and hit Enter, which will take you back to your standard system command prompt:

```
>>> exit()
C:\Users\nigel\OneDrive\Documents\mfdw_project>
```

Using the Interactive Interpreter with Django

Using the standard Python interactive interpreter is great for testing general Python code, but if you try to run any Django code from the Python prompt, you will get the error "`No module named 'django'`."

This is because Python has no knowledge of Django when you install it in a virtual environment, and because your Django project requires a few files loaded (particularly `settings.py`) to be able to run. Fortunately, Django's developers thought of this and provided a convenient management function that allows you to use the Python interpreter with Django.

First, start up your virtual environment like so:

```
C:\Users\...\mfdw_project> env_mfdw\scripts\activate
```

Then, change into your `mfdw_site` directory (type `cd mfdw_site` at the command prompt) and run the command `python manage.py shell`:

```
(env_mfdw) C:\Users\...\mfdw_project> cd mfdw_site
(env_mfdw) C:\Users\...mfdw_site> python manage.py shell

Python 3.7.0 (v3.7.0:1bf9cc5093, Jun 27 2018, 04:06:47)
[MSC v.1914 32 bit (Intel)] on win32
Type "help", "copyright", "credits" or "license" for more
information.
(InteractiveConsole)
>>>
```

This looks just the same as a Python prompt, but now you can access everything within your Django project. For example, your Project settings:

```
>>> from django.conf import settings
>>> settings.DEBUG
True
>>> settings.BASE_DIR
'C:\\Users\\nigel\\OneDrive\\Documents\\mfdw_project\\
mfdw_site'
>>> settings.LANGUAGE_CODE
'en-us'
```

If you want to see all the settings, type in:

```
dir(settings)  # Be warned, it's a long list!
```

There's not a lot more we can play with right now as your project is only an empty shell, but we will revisit the Django/Python interactive interpreter a few times in the book, so you will have plenty of chances to test it out.

Comments and Docstrings

Comments are common to most programming languages and are essential to describing code so you or other programmers can understand what is going on when the code is read in future.

Comments in Python are preceded by a hash (#) and a space:

```
# This is a comment.
```

Comments can be inline:

```
x = y+1   # This is an inline comment
```

Or single line:

```
# Define the list of guitarists
shredders = ["Kirk", "Dave", "Dimebag"]
```

Python doesn't have multi-line comments *per se*—you create multi-line comments by using multiple single line comments:

```
# This is the first line of the comment,
# This is the second line.
#
# You can create multi-paragraph comments by
# separating paragraphs with a line containing a single #
```

Docstrings are a special kind of string used by the Python compiler to create documentation automatically for your modules, classes, methods and functions.

A docstring is the first statement after the declaration of a module, class, method or function. They have two formats; single line:

```
"""This is a single line docstring"""
```

And multi-line:

```
"""This is a multi-line docstring.

The first line is a summary line, followed by a
blank line and then a more detailed description -
often describing arguments, return values, exceptions
raised and calling restrictions.

The summary statement can be on the same line as
the opening triple quotes or on the line below.

The closing triple quotes, however, must be on their
own line.
"""
```

The docstring becomes the __doc__ special attribute for the object which is used by many tools and applications, including Django's admin documentation tool, to create documentation for your code. For more information on docstrings, see **PEP 257**[3].

Math and Numbers

Python has a simple and straight forward approach to programming math and numbers—if you are OK with high school math, you will be OK with Python math. Carrying on from earlier examples, here are a few more using the Python interactive interpreter (don't type in the comments, I have added them for your information only):

---

3   https://www.python.org/dev/peps/pep-0257/

```
>>> 50 - 5*6          # Mathematical precedence
20                    # PEMDAS, BEDMAS or BODMAS
>>> (50 - 5) * 6      # depending which country you're from
270
>>> 2**10             # Power functions
1024
>>> import math       # Python math module
>>> r = 10
>>> area = math.pi*(r**2)        # Using pi
>>> area
314.1592653589793
>>> math.cos(math.radians(60))   # Trigonometry
0.5000000000000001
>>> math.log(256,2)              # logarithms
8.0
>>> import random                # Python random module
>>> random.random()
0.5362880665009504
>>> random.randrange(12)
11
>>> random.randrange(12)
4
>>>
```

There are dozens more functions you can use to do math and manipulate numbers in Python. For a list of all math functions, check out the Python documentation[4].

Strings

A string is simply a sequence of one or more characters—"a" is a string, "Hello There" is a string, if you were silly enough to load it all into a single variable, this whole book could be a string. String characters don't have to be printable—a string can contain any Unicode character.

Strings are *immutable*. An immutable object cannot be changed after it's created. I will be talking more about immutable and mutable objects shortly when I cover lists, tuples and dictionaries.

---

4   https://docs.python.org/3/library/math.html#module-math

To create a string, you simply enclose the string in single or double quotes:

```
x = 'Hello'
y = "There"
```

The only time it matters if you use single or double quotes is if there are quotes in the string:

```
a = 'This doesn't work'      # BAD, will break on
                             # quote in "doesn't"
b = "Wasn't that easy"       # GOOD
c = '"Air quotes" are silly' # Also GOOD
```

If there are multiple quotes in the string, you must escape the quotes with a backslash (\):

```
d = "Aren't quotes \"fun\"?"
```

Strings are a special class built in to Python, with many class methods available for working with them. Here are a few examples using the Python interactive interpreter:

```
>>> "hello".capitalize()     # Manipulate a string
                                directly
'Hello'                      # Capitalize string
>>> "hello".upper()          # Uppercase string
'HELLO'
>>> greet = "Hello There"    # Work with string
                                variable
>>> greet[0]                 # String indexing
'H'                          # First character
>>> greet[6]
'T'                          # Seventh character
>>> greet[:4]                # String slicing
'Hell'                       # First four characters
>>> greet[len(greet)-4:]
'here'                       # Last four characters
>>> greet[::-1]              # Reverse a string
'erehT olleH'
>>> padded = "    My name is Nige    "
>>> padded.lstrip()
```

```
'My name is Nige    '            # Removing whitespace
>>> padded.rstrip()
'    My name is Nige'
>>> greet.replace("e","_")       # Replacing characters
                                 # in a string
'H_llo Th_r_'
>>> greet.split()                # Splitting strings
['Hello', 'There']               # Default split is space
>>> greet.split("e")             # But can split on
                                 # anything
['H', 'llo Th', 'r', '']
>>>
```

Like math and numbers, this is only a small taste of what can be achieved with the string class. For more information see the Python string class documentation[5]

Formatting Strings

Another useful thing you can do with strings is to use *string interpolation* to substitute values into a formatted string. This is better explained with an example. Try this at the Python prompt:

```
>>> "There are %s apples left" % "four"
```

String interpolation is performed with the modulo (%) operator and takes the form:

```
format % values
```

So, when you enter the above code, Python replaces the string placeholder (%s) with the string "four". When you hit enter, Python prints out:

```
'There are four apples left'
>>>
```

---

5   https://docs.python.org/3/library/stdtypes.html#text-sequence-type-str

This works on multiple substitutions, however, with multiple substitutions the values must be passed in as a tuple (more on tuples shortly):

```
>>> "There are %s apples and %s oranges left" %
("four","two")
'There are four apples and two oranges left'
```

String formatting will substitute numbers as well. For example, %i will insert an integer:

```
>>> "There are %i apples and %i oranges left" % (2,7)
'There are 2 apples and 7 oranges left'
>>>
```

Other format strings include:

▶ **%X**. A signed hexadecimal (uppercase)

▶ **%f**. A floating point decimal

▶ **%c**. A single character

For more on formatting strings, see the Python documentation on String Formatting Operations[6].

Old and New Style String Formatting

Astute readers will note the string formatting footnote links to the Python 2 documentation. This is because most string substitution in Django uses the old-style `format % values` formatting. Python 2.6 introduced "new style" formatting, and then Python 3.6 added yet another with *formatted string literals*!

You can check out the new styles in the Python documentation in section 6.1.3—Format String Syntax[7].

---

6   https://docs.python.org/2/library/stdtypes.html#string-formatting
7   https://docs.python.org/3/library/string.html#format-string-syntax

Lists, Dictionaries and Tuples

Lists, dictionaries and tuples are used to store collections of objects. They are differentiated from each other by the delimiter they use:

▶ []. A **list**. E.g. `["one","two"]`

▶ {}. A **dictionary**. E.g. `{1:"one", 2:"two"}`

▶ (). A **tuple**. E.g. `("one", 2)`

Lists you should be very familiar with, as we all use lists daily. A dictionary is also straight forward—think of a regular dictionary where you have the word and then the meaning of the word. In Python, the word is called a *key* and the definition a *value*.

Tuples are like lists, with a couple of differences. Lists are designed to contain largely homogeneous data, much like in real life where you would have a shopping list or a to do list. By convention, Python list items should all be the same type (although Python doesn't enforce this rule).

Tuples, on the other hand, are used to store heterogeneous data— `("one", 2, [three])` is perfectly acceptable as a tuple, where it would be frowned upon as a list. A single element tuple (singleton) is also written differently to a single element list:

```
lst = ["one"]    # 1 element list
tpl = ("one",)   # 1 element tuple with trailing comma
                 # to differentiate between
                 # a plain string ("one") or a
                 # functions parameter some_func("one")
```

Tuples, like strings, are immutable. Once they are created you can't change them. Lists and dictionaries, however, are mutable and can be changed. Let me illustrate with some examples:

```
>>> lst = ["one"]    # Set up a list, tuple and dictionary
>>> tpl = ("one",)
>>> dict = {0:"one"}
```

```
>>> lst[0]           # All contain the same first element
'one'
>>> tpl[0]
'one'
>>> dict[0]
'one'
>>> lst[0] = "two"   # List is mutable (can be changed)
>>> lst
['two']
>>> dict[0] = "two" # So is the dictionary
>>> dict
{0: 'two'}
>>> tpl[0] = "two"   # Tuple is immutable. Can't change!
Traceback (most recent call last):
File "<stdin>", line 1, in <module>
TypeError: 'tuple' object does not support item
assignment

>>> str = "one"      # String is also immutable
>>> str[0] = "x"
Traceback (most recent call last):
File "<stdin>", line 1, in <module>
TypeError: 'str' object does not support item assignment
```

One last point on tuples *vs.* lists—tuples are often used for homogeneous data that the programmer doesn't want changed by accident. So, if you have a list of items that should not be changed, it can be a good idea to use a tuple instead of a list.

The if Statement and Code Branching

Python, like most programming languages, has an if statement that provides branching in your code. The syntax of Python's if statement is as follows:

```
if [expression is True]:
    # execute this code when True
else:
    # execute this code when False
```

The else branch is optional:

```
if [expression is True]:
    # only executes when True
# resume code execution
```

The expression can be anything that evaluates to True or False. A few examples:

1. if num >= 10:
2. if str == "Hello:
3. if this != that:
4. if SomeVar:

...and so on.

Take note of example 4 above—in Python, anything that does not equate to zero, Null, or an empty object is True. For example:

```
>>> s = 0
>>> if s:
...       print("True")
...     # Python returns nothing - statement is false
>>> s = 1
>>> if s:
...       print("True")
...
True
>>> s = ""
>>> if s:
...       print("True")
...     # Nothing again - statement is false
>>> s = "Hello"
>>> if s:
...       print("True")
...
True
```

Python includes a comprehensive range of boolean operators that you can use within your expressions:

▶ `<`. Less than

▶ `<=`. Less than or equal

▶ `>`. Greater than

▶ `>=`. Greater than or equal

▶ `==`. Equal

▶ `!=`. Not equal

▶ **is**. Is a particular object

▶ **is not**. Isn't a particular object

Boolean operations are also supported for negating and chaining expressions:

▶ **or**. Either expression can be `True`

▶ **and**. Both expressions must be `True`

▶ **not**. Negate the proceeding expression

Python also supports multiple branching using the `elif` (short for "else if") statement:

```
if [expl is True]:
    # execute if expl is True
elif [exp2 is True]:
    # execute if exp2 is True
elif [exp3 is True]:
    # execute if exp3 is True
# and so on ...
```

Loops and Iterators

Loops and iterators both do the same basic thing—repeat a section of code until some condition is met. With a loop, the repetition can be any arbitrary code sequence, whereas an iterator steps through an *iterable* object. An iterable object is an object that can be indexed (stepped through) in a sequential way. The most common iterable types in Python are the sequence types—strings, lists, tuples and ranges.

The While Loop

To create a program loop in Python, you use the `while` statement. For example, here is a very simple loop:

```
a = 1
while a < 5:
    print(a)
    a+=1
```

This should be easy to follow:

1. Set the value of a to 1;
2. Start a loop with the `while` statement;
3. Print out the current value of a;
4. Increment a; and
5. Repeat while the expression "a < 5" is True.

If you run this code at the Python prompt, your output should look like this:

```
>>> a = 1
>>> while a < 5:
...        print(a)
...        a+=1
...
1
2
3
4
>>>
```

What if I leave out "a+=1"?

If you think about it, if you don't increment a the expression a < 5 will never be False—the loop will go on printing a = 1 forever (or until you interrupt the code execution). This is what's called an infinite loop, or a loop that will never exit.

Accidentally creating an infinite loop is common—both among beginning and experienced programmers. If you ever have a Python program that just seems to stop and go nowhere, odds are you have an infinite loop somewhere in your code.

Python's while loops are very useful and can be used for much more than simple tasks like printing out a variable. For example, the factorial (!) of any number is simply the multiplication of the number with all the preceding integers (so 4! is equal to 1*2*3*4). Here's how to calculate the factorial of 9 with a while loop:

```
fact, mul = 1, 2     # Multiple assignment
while mul < 10:
    fact, mul = fact*mul, mul + 1
    print(fact)
```

In the first line I am using multiple assignment, which is a useful feature of Python's programming syntax. The statement fact, mul = 1, 2 is a shorthand way of writing:

```
fact = 1
mul = 2
```

Line 3 is where all the magic happens. First, we multiply the current value of fact by mul and then we increment mul by 1. We then print out the new value of fact. If you run this at the Python prompt, you should see something like this:

```
>>> fact, mul = 1, 2
>>> while mul < 10:
...     fact, mul = fact*mul, mul + 1
...     print(fact)
```

```
...
2
6
24
120
720
5040
40320
362880
>>>
```

Breaking out of Loops

The break and continue statements allow you to exit a loop before the loop condition is met. Consider the following code:

```
a, b = 1, 1
while a < 5:
    print("a =", a)
    a +=1
    while b < 5:
        print("b =", b)
        if b == 2:
            b = 1
            break
        b +=1
```

The break statement will only exit the currently running loop, so in the above example the break statement only exits the inner while loop. Let's see what the output is when we run this code:

```
>>> a,b = 1,1
>>> while a < 5:
...         print("a =", a)
...         a +=1
...         while b < 5:
...             print("b =", b)
...             if b == 2:
...                 b = 1
...                 break
...             b +=1
```

```
...
a = 1
b = 1
b = 2
a = 2
b = 1
b = 2
a = 3
b = 1
b = 2
a = 4
b = 1
b = 2
>>>
```

You can see that the break statement doesn't affect the outer loop—it continues to run until "a < 5" is False. Because the inner loop always breaks when b is equal to 2, the inner while loop never completes.

The continue statement, on the other hand, won't execute any of the code after the continue, but instead it jumps to the next iteration of the loop. Consider the following code:

```
a = 0
while a < 5:
    a+=1
    if a == 3:
        print("My favorite number is", a)
        continue      # Go to next iteration of loop
    print("a =", a) # The continue statement will stop
                    # this from printing when a equals 3
```

Run this code and you should see a different string printed when a equals 3:

```
>>> a = 0
>>> while a < 5:
...     a+=1
...     if a == 3:
...         print("My favorite number is", a)
...         continue
```

```
...         print("a =", a)
...
a = 1
a = 2
My favorite number is 3
a = 4
a = 5
>>>
```

The break and continue statements can also be used inside a for loop.

Iterating with a For Loop

The for loop is designed to step through an iterable item. It takes the basic form:

```
for [item] in [iterable]:
```

As I said earlier in the chapter, the most common iterables are strings, lists, tuples and ranges. Here are some examples:

```
>>> word = "Hello"
>>> for char in word:    # Step through each character
...         print(char)      # in the word
...
...
H
e
l
l
o
>>> lst = ["1","2","3"] # Step through each item
>>> for item in lst:     # in the list
...         print(item)
...
...
1
2
3
>>> tup = (1,"two", 3)   # Step through each item
>>> for item in tup:     # in the tuple
...         print(item)
...
...
```

```
1
two
3
>>> for i in range(5):   # The range function provides you
...     print(i)          # with a sequence of integers
...
0
1
2
3
4
>>>
```

This should be easy to follow. The range() function we haven't covered, but it's basically an easy way of creating a sequence of numbers. More on the range() function in the Python documentation[8].

Catching Errors

Let's say you have a simple function where you need to take the answer from a previous operation and divide it by 5:

```
ans = answer/5
print("Answer divided by 5 is", ans)
```

Seems straight forward, let's try that out at the Python prompt:

```
>>> answer = 3
>>> ans = answer/5
>>> print("Answer divided by 5 is", ans)
Answer divided by 5 is 0.6
>>>
```

So far, so good—but what if, instead of getting an integer, our function got handed a string? Let's try that again in Python:

```
>>> answer = "3"
>>> ans = 5/answer
```

```
Traceback (most recent call last):
File "<stdin>", line 1, in <module>
TypeError: unsupported operand type(s) for /: 'int' and
'str'
```

Oops! You will note that you didn't even get to enter the final print() statement before Python threw an error. If this happened in the middle of an important part of your code, it could crash your program with potentially disastrous results.

Luckily, Python provides an easy, but robust way of handling errors within your code with the try ... except statement:

```
try:
    # Try this piece of code
except:
    # On error, execute this bit of code.
```

Let's try that now with our previous example:

```
>>> answer = 3
>>> try:
...     ans = answer/5 # Try to execute this statement
...     print("Answer divided by 5 is", ans)
... except:
...     print("something went wrong")
...
Answer divided by 5 is 0.6
# In this case, all is OK and we get the expected output

>>> answer = "3"
>>> try:
...     ans = answer/5 # Passing a string throws an error
...     print("Answer divided by 5 is", ans)
... except:
...     print("something went wrong")
...
something went wrong
# Python captures the error and lets us know
```

This code is better, but we still have no idea what caused the error. Lucky for us, Python also captures the type of error. If you look closely at the first bit of code that threw the error, you will see this line:

```
TypeError: unsupported operand type(s) for /: 'int' and
'str'
```

In this case, Python is telling us that the bad input is throwing a TypeError. So let's modify the code to make it a bit more descriptive:

```
>>> answer = "3"
>>> try:
...      ans = answer/5
...      print("Answer divided by 5 is", ans)
... except TypeError:
...      print("Type Error. Answer must be an integer.")
...
Type Error. Answer must be an integer.
>>>
```

This is only a very basic example of error handling. It's also incomplete (the code above will still crash if answer is zero); however, more complex implementations of the try...except statement build on these fundamentals.

For more on the try...except statement, see errors and exceptions[9] in the Python documentation. You can also find a comprehensive list of built-in exceptions[10] in the Python docs.

Classes and Functions

The basic purpose of classes and functions is to group together pieces of related code. The major difference between the two is that a function *does* something whereas a class *is* something. For example, if Person was a class, walk() and eat() would be functions.

---

9   https://docs.python.org/3/tutorial/errors.html#errors-and-exceptions
10   https://docs.python.org/3/library/exceptions.html#built-in-exceptions

Both classes and functions can contain other functions. If a function is inside another function, it's called a *sub-function*. If a function is included inside a class, it's called a *method*. Subclasses also exist, but they are created by a process called *inheritance*. We will get to inheritance in just a bit.

To define a function in Python, you use the `def` statement:

```
def function_name([parameter list]):
    # rest of function
```

To define a class in Python, you use the `class` statement:

```
class Someclass([argument list]):
    # class constructor
    __init__():
        # Constructor code
    # class methods
    def ...
```

You create subclasses that contain all the attributes and methods of another class using inheritance. Inheritance is an important concept in object-oriented programming. Inheritance helps prevent repetition in code, and it allows programmers to build complex programs from simpler building blocks.

To create a class that inherits from another class, you refer to the parent when defining the class:

```
class ChildClass(ParentClass):
```

This is easier to understand with an example—a simple Django form class:

```
class ContactForm(forms.Form):
    subject = forms.CharField(max_length=100)
    email = forms.EmailField(required=False)
    message = forms.CharField(widget=forms.Textarea)
```

In this example, the class is inheriting from Django's `forms.Form` class, which make all the methods and attributes of the parent class (`forms.Form`) available in the child class (subclass) `ContactForm`.

More on Classes and Functions

This very brief introduction to classes and functions only scratches the surface of their full capabilities. The aim is simply to introduce them in a way that you will recognize what they are while you are learning Django. As Django uses classes and functions extensively, you will have plenty of opportunity to pick up more skills and understanding as you go.

Packages and Modules

To clearly organize large projects into logical units, Python structures code into modules and packages.

A module is the base unit of Python's program structure. A module is a file with a `.py` extension that contains all the functions, classes and definitions pertaining to that module.

A package is a collection of modules all saved inside a package folder. The package folder must contain a file called `__init__.py` for Python to be able to identify the folder as a package.

Let's have a look at the Django project we created in the last chapter to see packages and modules in action:

```
\mfdw_site
__init__.py     # This tells Python that
                # mfdw_site is a package.
settings.py     # The settings module for our project.
urls.py         # The urls module for our project.
# ...
```

The Dot Operator

Dot notation is a common idiom in object-oriented programming. I like to think of the dot like a point because the dot *points* to something. In the case of Python, the dot operator points to the next object in the object chain. In Django classes, the object chain is like this:

```
package.module.class.method
```

Or in the case of functions:

```
package.module.function.attribute
```

Some real-life examples:

▶ `forms.Form` points to the `Form` class in the `forms` package.

▶ `pages.apps.PagesConfig` points to the `PagesConfig` class in the apps sub-package of the `pages` package. I.e., the `apps.py` file in you pages app.

▶ `django.conf.urls` points to the `urls` package inside the `conf` package inside `django` which is also a `Python` package!

This can sometimes get a bit confusing, but if you remember to join the dots (sorry, bad pun there), you can usually find out what the dot operator is referring to.

Regular Expressions

While not strictly a Python topic, it's important to introduce regular expressions (or regexes), as they are used quite often by Django. While there are dozens of regex symbols and patterns, you'll probably only use a few in practice. Table 5-1 lists a selection of common symbols.

Table 5-1. *Common regex symbols*

Symbol	Matches
`. (dot)`	Any single character
`\d`	Any single digit
`[A-Z]`	Any character between A and Z (uppercase)
`[a-z]`	Any character between a and z (lowercase)
`[A-Za-z]`	Any character between a and z (case-insensitive)
`+`	One or more of the previous expression (e.g., `\d+` matches one or more digits)
`[^/]+`	One or more characters until (and not including) a forward slash
`?`	Zero or one of the previous expression (e.g., `\d?` matches zero or one digits)
`*`	Zero or more of the previous expression (e.g., `\d*` matches zero, one or more than one digit)
`{1,3}`	Between one and three (inclusive) of the previous expression (e.g., `\d{1,3}` matches one, two or three digits)
`(...)`	Matches whatever regular expression is inside the parentheses and indicates the start and end of a group
`(?P<name>...)`	Matches whatever regular expression is inside the parentheses and turns matched data into a named parameter. E.g. `(?P<pk>[0-9]+)` would insert any captured digits into a parameter named `pk`.

For more on regular expressions, see the Python regex documentation[11].

---

11   https://docs.python.org/3.7/library/re.html

Chapter Summary

In this chapter we covered the Python programming language—learning about how Python programs are structured, the syntax of the Python programming language and many of the more common language elements and functions in Python.

With a thorough grounding in writing Python code, it's now time to move on to writing your very first Django application, which is exactly what we are going to do in the next chapter.

6

Your First Django Application

You will remember from Chapter 3 that Django uses the Model–Template–View (MTV) design pattern. The process flow of MTV is as follows:

1. The **Model** retrieves data from the database, which is requested by the;
2. **View**, which applies any business logic and formatting to the model data and then sends the packaged and formatted data to the;
3. **Template**, which then renders the data with any display logic necessary.

In this chapter, we will start by creating a very simple view and a urls.py file for our app to demonstrate how Django's navigation works. In the next chapter, we will create our Pages model and we will visit the admin for the first time so we can add some content to our pages.

Following that, in Chapter 8 we will dress up the site with templates and then in Chapter 9, we will modify our urls.py to display page content from the database.

Before we get to creating our first view, however, we need to dig a little deeper into our Django project's structure to better understand how the pieces fit together and then create the key component that makes the MTV pattern work—a Django *application*.

Django Project Structure

Let's take a closer look at what Django has created for us so far. Open your project folder (`mfdw_project`). The folder structure should look like this:

```
\env_mfdw
\mfdw_site
    db.sqlite3
    manage.py
    \mfdw_site
            __init.py__
            settings.py
            urls.py
            wsgi.py
```

Let's examine these files and folders in more detail:

▶ The **env_mfdw** folder is where the files for your virtual environment are stored. There are lots of interesting goodies in here for advanced users, but as a beginner it's best you leave everything inside this folder alone.

▶ The **outer mfdw_site** folder is merely a container for your project. While the `startproject` command created the folder, Django doesn't care about the folder name, so you can rename it to something meaningful to you.

▶ Inside the outer `mfdw_site` folder are two files:

  ▷ **db.sqlite3**. The database created when you ran the `migrate` command; and

  ▷ **manage.py**. A command-line utility for executing Django commands from within your project.

▶ The **inner mfdw_site** folder is your Django project. The `__init__.py` file within this folder tells Python that this folder is a Python package (see Chapter 5).

▶ **settings.py** contains the setting for your project (see below for more on settings).

- **`urls.py`** contains project-level URL declarations. By default, this contains a single URL pattern for the admin. We will be covering URLs in more detail later in the chapter.

- **`wsgi.py`** enables WSGI compatible web servers to serve your project. This file is only used in deployment, so is out of the scope of this book.

Django Settings

The `settings.py` file contains the configuration information for your Django project. When you ran `startproject`, Django created a number of common settings with default values for you. There are a large number of settings available—core settings for database configuration, caching, email, file uploads and globalization, as well as a range of additional settings for authentication, messaging, sessions and static file handling.

We will only be covering a very small subset of the available settings in this book. For a complete reference, see the Django website[1].

Django Applications

You might have noticed that there is no real program code in your project so far—you have a settings file with configuration information, an almost empty URLs file and a command-line utility that launches a website that doesn't really do anything.

This is because, to create a functioning Django website, you need to create Django applications.

A Django application (or app for short) is where the work is done. Good design practice says that each Django app should do one thing—a blog, or article directory or music collection, etc. A Django project is the collection of apps and configuration settings that make up a Django website.

---

1   https://docs.djangoproject.com/en/2.1/ref/settings/

Apps are one of Django's killer features. Not only do they allow you to add functionality to a Django project without interfering with other parts of the website, but apps are designed to be portable, so you can use one app in multiple projects.

Creating the Pages App

Before creating our first app, we need to make one important change to the project folders—rename the outer \mfdw_site directory.

A very common complaint I hear from programmers just starting out with Django is how confusing it is to know which folder they should be working in when there are two folders named the same.

As I said a couple of pages ago, Django doesn't care what you name this folder—so let's go ahead and break thirteen years of Django tutorial convention and actually rename the folder! In this case, we are going to rename it to "mfdw_root".

Once you have made the change, your folder structure should go from this:

```
\mfdw_project
    \mfdw_site
            \mfdw_site
```

To this:

```
\mfdw_project
    \mfdw_root
            \mfdw_site
```

Now we have cleared up any potential confusion, let's go ahead and create our first Django app.

If you have ever used a content management system, or visit websites with multiple sources of information, you may have noticed that they often break their content up into broad categories—pages for site-related information, articles for news and periodic information and maybe even blogs where contributors post shorter, more personal content.

We won't be going into such detail in this introductory book, but we will create a simple but practical website—one that displays a few pages of information about our fictitious company Meandco Web Design. Since we want to display pages of information, lets call our app something practical—pages.

Return to the virtual environment command prompt (make sure you are in the mfdw_root directory) and enter:

```
(env_mfdw) ...\mfdw_root>python manage.py startapp pages
```

Your project directory should now look like this:

```
\mfdw_project
    \mfdw_root
            \mfdw_site
            \pages
            db.sqlite3
            manage.py
```

Notice that your new pages app is in the same directory as manage.py, not inside the mfdw_site folder. It's important that you get this right, otherwise you will get "no module named 'pages'" errors when trying to run code later in this book.

If you do make a mistake, it's very easy to fix. Delete the \pages folder out of the \mfdw_site folder, open the command window in \mfdw_root and run the startapp utility again.

Once you have created your app, you have to tell Django to install it into your project. This is easy to do—inside your settings.py file is a list named INSTALLED_APPS. This list contains all the apps that are installed in your Django project. Django comes with a few apps pre-installed, we just have to add your new pages app to the list:

```
1   INSTALLED_APPS = [
2       'pages.apps.PagesConfig',
3       'django.contrib.admin',
4       # more apps
5   ]
```

Inside every app, Django creates a file, apps.py, that contains a configuration class named after your app. In this case, the class is named PagesConfig. To register our app with Django, we need to point to the PagesConfig class—which is exactly what we are doing in line 2 or our modified INSTALLED_APPS list.

If you were wondering, PagesConfig by default contains a single configuration option—the name of the app ("pages").

Line Numbers in Listings

Throughout this book, I will be using line numbers on more complex sections of code. The line numbers are there for you to more easily identify which sections of code I am explaining in the text.

If you are using a text editor that displays line numbers, note that **in most cases the line number in the listing will not be the same as the line number in the actual file**.

Django App Structure

Now let's have a closer look at the structure of our new pages app:

```
\pages
   \migrations
   __init__.py
   admin.py
   apps.py
   models.py
   tests.py
   views.py
```

▶ The **migrations** folder is where Django stores migrations, or changes to your database. There's nothing in here you need to worry about.

▶ **__init__.py** tells Python that your pages app is a package.

▶ **admin.py** is where you register your models with the Django admin application.

▶ **apps.py** is a configuration file common to all Django apps.

▶ **models.py** is where the models for your app are located.

▶ **tests.py** contains test procedures that will be run when testing your app. Testing is a more advanced topic which won't be covered in this book.

▶ **views.py** is where the views for your app are located.

You will notice that most of these files are either empty, or only have a couple of lines of code in them. This is because Django's startproject and startapp utilities only create the bare minimum framework from which to build a Django website. Django adds no boilerplate, no cruft and no unnecessary code, leaving you with a simple, clean framework that you can build on to create exactly what you want.

It should also be noted that you can create all the files and folders for a Django website manually if you wish. While the structure created by startproject and startapp is very common, it's not the only way to structure a Django website.

As your programming career progresses, you will find there are several popular ways of structuring a Django project. The key takeaway for you now, however, is that Django doesn't care how you structure your project, which is another big plus for Django's flexibility.

Your First View

Project Files

The following code examples assume that you have automatically created all your project and app files with the **startproject** and **startapp** utilities. It's recommended you use this default structure throughout the book so that your code matches the examples. Also note, the code in this book was generated with Django 2.1, so the default file contents may be slightly different if you are using a later version.

To create our first view, we need to modify the `views.py` file in our `pages` app (changes in bold):

```
# \mfdw_site\pages\views.py

1   from django.shortcuts import render
2   from django.http import HttpResponse
3
4   def index(request):
5       return HttpResponse("<h1>The Meandco Homepage</h1>")
```

Let's examine this code closely:

▶ **Line 1.** Imports the `render` method. This is added to the file automatically by `startapp`. `render()` is used when rendering templates, which we will be covering in Chapter 8.

▶ **Line 2.** We import the `HttpResponse` method. HTTP, the communication protocol used by all web browsers, uses *request* and *response* objects to pass data to and from your app and the browser. We need a response object to be able to pass view information back to the browser.

▶ **Lines 4 and 5.** This is your view function. This is an example of a *function-based* view. It takes a request from your web browser and returns a response. In this simple case, it's just a line of text formatted as an HTML heading.

Take careful note of the name for your view. It's a historical convention that the root page (home page) of a website is named `index.html`. For example, `http://www.example.com/` would actually point to `http://www.example.com/index.html`. I follow this convention by naming the home page view "index". Feel free to go against convention if you must, but be prepared for someone to ask *"where is your index view?"*.

Configuring the URLs

If you started the development server now, you would notice that it still displays the welcome page. This is because, in order for Django to use your new view, you need to tell Django this is the view you want displayed when someone navigates to the site root (home page). We do this by configuring our URLs.

In Django, the `path()` function is used to configure URLs. In its basic form, the `path()` function has a very simple syntax:

```
path(route, view)
```

A practical example of the basic `path()` function would be:

```
path('mypage/', views.myview)
```

In this example, a request to `http://example.com/mypage` would be routed to the `myview` function in the application's `views.py` file. Don't worry if this is a bit confusing right now, it will make a lot more sense once you have written a couple of views.

The `path()` function also takes an optional `name` parameter and any number of additional keyword arguments passed as a Python dictionary. We will get to these more advanced options a bit later in the book.

The `path()` function statements are kept in a special file called `urls.py`.

When startproject created our website, it created a urls.py file in our site folder (\mfdw_site\urls.py). This is a good place for site-wide navigation, but is rarely a good place to put URLs relating to individual applications. Not only is having all our URLs in the one file more complex and less portable, but can lead to strange behavior if two applications use a view with the same name.

To solve this problem, we create a new urls.py file for each application. If you are wondering why startapp didn't create the file for us, not all apps have public views that are accessible via URL. A utility program that does background tasks, for example, would not need a urls.py file. Remember, Django doesn't assume anything, so it lets you decide whether your app needs its own urls.py file.

First, we need to create a new urls.py file in our pages app:

```
# \mfdw_root\pages\urls.py

1  from django.urls import path
2  from . import views
3
4  urlpatterns = [
5      path('', views.index, name='index'),
6  ]
```

Let's look at this code closer:

▶ **Line 1.** Imports the path() function. This import is necessary for the URL dispatcher to work and is common to all urls.py files.

▶ **Line 2.** Imports the local views.py file. The dot operator (".") in this case is shorthand for the current package, so this is saying "import all views from the current package (pages)".

▶ **Line 4.** Lists the URL patterns registered for this app. For readability, the list is broken into multiple lines, with one URL pattern per line.

▶ **Line 5.** Is the actual URL dispatcher:

▷ '**'**. Matches an empty string. It will also match the "/" as Django automatically removes the slash. In other words, this matches both `http://example.com` and `http://example.com/`.

▷ **views.index**. Points to our `index` view. I.e., the dot operator is pointing to the `index` view inside the `views.py` file that we imported in Line 2.

Now let's look at the changes to our site `urls.py` file:

```
# \mfdw_site\urls.py

1  from django.urls import include, path
2  from django.contrib import admin
3
4  urlpatterns = [
5      path('admin/', admin.site.urls),
6      path('', include('pages.urls')),
7  ]
```

We have made a couple of important changes to the file:

▶ **Line 1.** We have added the `include()` function to our imports.

▶ **Line 6.** We have added a new URL dispatcher. In this file, the dispatcher is simply including the `urls.py` file from the `pages` app. The empty string (`''`) will match everything after the domain name. **NOTE:** This pattern must be the last entry in `urlpatterns` list. The reason for this will become apparent in a later chapter.

If you now run the development server, and navigate to `http://127.0.0.1:8000/` in your browser, you should see a plain, but functioning home page (Figure 6-1).

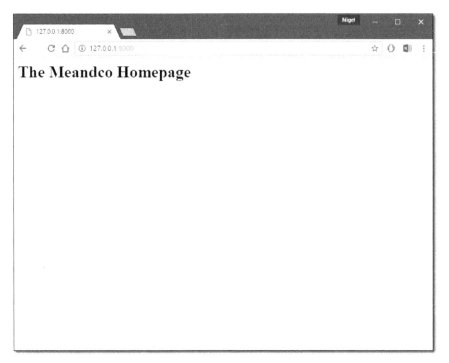

Figure 6-1. *A very plain, but functioning home page for your website.*

So What Just Happened?

To better understand how Django works, let's build on the generic example from Chapter 3 with a concrete example of what Django did to display our home page:

1. Our browser sent a message to the Django development server requesting it return content located at the root URL (`http://127.0.0.1:8000/`).

2. Django then looked for a URL pattern that matches the request, by first searching the site level `urls.py` and then each of the apps for a `urls.py` file containing a pattern that matches.

3. Django checks the first pattern (`^admin/`) in our site level `urls.py` which doesn't match, and moves on to the second line in which the empty string (root URL) matches.

4. The matching pattern includes the `urls.py` from the `pages` app. Basically this include says "go look in the `pages` app for a pattern that matches".

5. Once in the app-level `urls.py`, the empty string matches again, but this time the request is sent to the `index` view.

6. The `index` view then renders our simple HTML message to a `HttpResponse` that is sent to the browser.

7. The browser renders the response and we see our page heading.

Every Django application follows this same basic process each time it receives a request from the browser.

Chapter Summary

In this chapter, we used the `startapp` helper function to create our first Django application (app). We then modified some key files in the Django app to create a static webpage that renders a simple message in the browser.

In the next chapter, we will create a Django model to contain the content for each of our site pages. We will also visit Django's admin app for the first time and create some pages and content for our site.

7

Creating the Page Model

As we discussed in Chapter 3, a Django model is a data object that maps your app's data to the database without you having to know SQL, or how the underlying database structures your data. Each of your app's models are a class that you create in your app's models.py file.

The Page Model

The easiest way to learn how models work is to create one—so let's go ahead and create a Page model:

```
# \mfdw_root\pages\models.py

1   from django.db import models
2
3   class Page(models.Model):
4       title = models.CharField(max_length=60)
5       permalink = models.CharField(max_length=12,
    unique=True)
6       update_date = models.DateTimeField('Last Updated')
7       bodytext = models.TextField('Page Content',
    blank=True)
```

Now let's take a closer look at your first model, as a fair bit is going on here:

▶ **Line 1**. Import the models package from django.db. If you used startapp, this line will be in your file.

▸ **Line 3**. Create the `Page` class, which must inherit from Django's `Model` class.

▸ **Lines 4 to 7**. Define the fields for the model. These fields will have a corresponding field in the table that Django creates for the model in the database:

  ▷ **title**. The title of your page. This will be put in the `<title></title>` element of your template (see Chapter 8).

  ▷ **permalink**. A permalink to an individual page. This will make more sense in Chapter 9 when we write new URLs to access your pages.

  ▷ **update_date**. The date the page was last updated. Use this field to keep track of page edits.

  ▷ **bodytext**. The HTML content of your page. This will be put in the `<body></body>` element of your template (see Chapter 8).

Each of our model fields has a related Django *field type* and *field options*. The `Page` model uses three different field types—`CharField`, `DateTimeField` and `TextField`. Let's have a look at the field types and options in more detail:

▸ **title**. A `CharField` is a short line of text (up to 255 characters). In this case, the `max_length` option sets the maximum length of the page title to 60 characters.

▸ **permalink**. As in the `title` field, the permalink field has a `max_length` option set, but for the permalink, the length is limited to 12. `permalink` also has an additional option—`unique=True`. As we are using the permalink to create a URL to the page, we don't want the permalink to be duplicated, so this option ensures that an error will be thrown if you try to enter the same permalink for two pages.

▸ **update_date**. A `DateTimeField` records a Python `datetime` object. Many model fields allow you to set a string as the first option for the *verbose name* of a field. This verbose name is used to create a human-friendly name for the model field. In the case of `update_date`, we are setting this name to "Last Updated". Most commonly used for displaying human-friendly field names in the admin.

▶ **bodytext**. A `TextField` is a large text field that can hold many thousands of characters (maximum depends on the database). Sets the verbose name to "Page Content". The final option—`blank=True`—is set so that we can create a page without any content. The default for this option is `False`, so if you didn't add any page content, Django will throw an error.

We have only covered a few field types and options in our first model, we will cover a few more in Chapter 11. If you want to have a go creating models now with different field types and options, there are reference tables for common field types and options in the Appendix starting on page 251.

There is one more thing we have to do with our model—for a model to be accessible from the admin, it needs to be registered. Registering and configuring a model for the admin is done by adding code to the app's `admin.py` file (changes in bold):

```
# \mfdw_root\pages\admin.py

1   from django.contrib import admin
2   from .models import Page
3
4   admin.site.register(Page)
```

We have added two lines of code to our `admin.py` file:

▶ **Line 2.** We import the `Page` model

▶ **Line 4.** We register the `Page` model with the admin

Very simple. Now we just have to create a migration for the `pages` app, so Django can add the model to the database. Return to your virtual environment command prompt (exit the development server if it's still running) and enter:

```
(env_mfdw)... >python manage.py makemigrations pages
```

The output should look like this:

```
Migrations for 'pages':
  pages\migrations\0001_initial.py:
    - Create model page
```

Then we need to perform the migration:

```
(env_mfdw) ...\mfdw_root>python manage.py migrate
```

The output from this command should look like this:

```
Operations to perform:
  Apply all migrations: admin, auth, contenttypes, pages,
sessions
Running migrations:
  Applying pages.0001_initial... OK
```

If this doesn't work and Django complains that it can't find your pages app, this is almost certainly because you forgot to add the pages app to your INSTALLED_APPS in Chapter 6 (see page 86).

And we are done. Now it's time to move on to the admin so we can add some content to our pages.

A First Look at the Django Admin

For most modern websites, an *administrative interface* (or admin for short) is an essential part of the infrastructure. This is a web-based interface, limited to trusted site administrators, that enables an admin to add, edit and delete site content.

Other examples include the interface you use to post to your blog, the backend site managers use to moderate user-generated comments or the tool your clients use to update the press releases on a website you built for them.

Django comes with a built-in admin interface—with Django's admin you can authenticate users, display and handle forms and validate input; all automatically. Django also provides a convenient interface to our models, which is what we will use now to add content to our pages app.

Using the Admin Site

When you ran startproject in Chapter 4, Django created and configured the default admin site for you. All that you need to do is create an admin user (superuser) to log into the admin site. To create an admin user, run the following command from inside your virtual environment:

```
python manage.py createsuperuser
```

Enter your desired username and press enter.

```
Username: admin
```

You will then be prompted for your email address:

```
Email address: admin@example.com
```

The final step is to enter your password. You will be asked to enter your password twice, the second time as a confirmation of the first.

```
Password: **********
Password (again): *********
Superuser created successfully.
```

Now that you have created an admin user, you're ready to start using the Django admin. Let's start the development server and explore.

First, make sure the development server is running, then open a web browser to http://127.0.0.1:8000/admin/. You should see the admin's login screen (Figure 7-1).

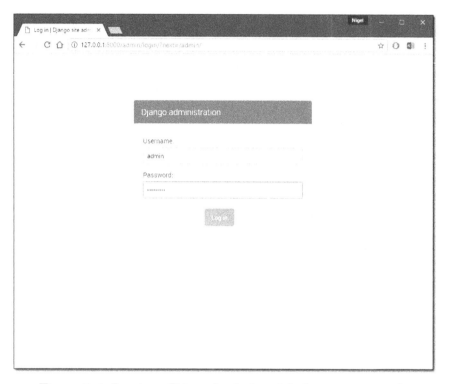

Figure 7-1. *Log in to Django's admin with the username and password you just created.*

Since translation is turned on by default, the login screen may be displayed in your own language, depending on your browser's settings and on whether Django has a translation for your language.

Log in with the administrator account you created. Once logged in, you should see the Django admin index page (Figure 7-2).

At the top of the index page is the **Authentication and Authorization** group with two types of editable content: **Groups** and **Users**. They are provided by the authentication framework included in Django. We will be looking at users and groups in Chapter 13.

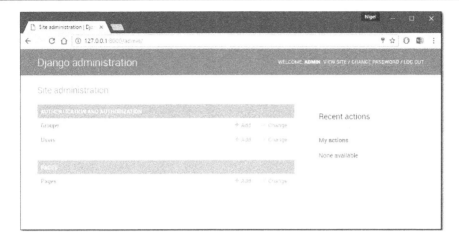

Figure 7-2. The admin home page lists your registered models as well as a couple of extras created by Django.

Beneath the Authentication and Authorization group is a group added by the admin for our `Page` model. We will be using this group to add some page content to our site, so go ahead and click the **Add** link next to the green cross on the right of the **Pages** entry.

The admin site is designed to be used by non-technical users, and as such it should be self-explanatory. Nevertheless, let's cover a few of the basic features. Each type of data in the Django admin site has a *change list* and an *edit form*.

Change lists show you all available objects in the database, and edit forms let you add, change or delete records in your database. Figure 7-3 shows the edit form that opened when you clicked the **Add** link.

As you are adding a record, the edit form is blank, allowing you to enter new information into the database. Fill out the fields as follows:

- ▶ **Title:**   Meandco Home
- ▶ **Permalink**:   /

▶ **Last Updated:**   Enter any date and time

▶ **Page Content:**   Enter some content

When entering the page content, remember that it needs to be HTML to display well in your browser. At this stage, a heading and a few paragraphs is OK. Don't go crazy here creating page content because, when we deploy the site in Chapter 14, you will lose all the content. If you need help with HTML, the HTML tutorial on W3schools is a great resource[1].

Figure 7-3. Add a new page to your Page model using the Django admin.

Also note that our edit form is using the **Last Updated** and **Page Content** verbose field names we entered when we created the Page model.

---

1   https://www.w3schools.com/html/

Now that you have entered the information for your home page, click **Save and add another** down the bottom right of your screen. Add two more pages (**Last Updated** and **Page Content** can be whatever you like):

1. **Title:** About Us; **Permalink:** /about
2. **Title:** Services; **Permalink:** /services

Once you have entered the information for your services page, click **SAVE** rather than **Save and add another**. This will take you to the Pages change list (Figure 7-4). The Pages change list can also be accessed from the admin index page by clicking Pages on the left of the group, or by clicking the second Pages link in the breadcrumbs on the top right of the edit page.

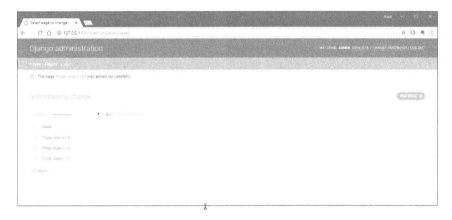

Figure 7-4. The new pages have been added to the database, but the page names are not very helpful.

Notice that, while the change list contains three page entries, they are named (unhelpfully) "Page object". This is because we haven't told the admin what to call our Page objects.

This is an easy fix. Go back to your models.py file and make the changes in bold:

```
# \mfdw_root\pages\models.py

1  from django.db import models
2
3  class Page(models.Model):
4      title = models.CharField(max_length=60)
5      permalink = models.CharField(max_length=12,
   unique=True)
6      update_date = models.DateTimeField('Last Updated')
7      bodytext = models.TextField('Page Content',
   blank=True)
8
9      def __str__(self):
10          return self.title
```

So, what did we do here? In lines 9 and 10, we have created a new class method. The `__str__` method is a special method that returns a human-readable version of the `Pages` class whenever Python asks for a string representation of the `Pages` object (which is what the admin is doing). If there is no `__str__` method, Python returns the object type—hence "Page object".

In our modified `models.py`, we are simply returning the page title. Refresh the admin screen and you should see a somewhat more useful change list for our pages (Figure 7-5).

There's one final thing we want to do with the Pages list display. While we now have the page titles listed, there is still some work to do to make the list display more useful:

1. We want to see when each page was last updated to keep track of changes to our site;

2. We want to display the page titles in alphabetical order to make them easier to browse; and

3. Once there are many pages, we want a handy way to search for a page.

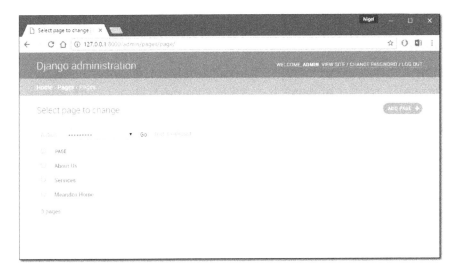

Figure 7-5. *With a small change to our Page class, the admin now shows the correct page names.*

In Django, these changes are very easy to do—you simply add a new class to your admin.py file (changes in bold):

```
# \mfdw_root\pages\admin.py

1  from django.contrib import admin
2  from .models import Page
3
4  class PageAdmin(admin.ModelAdmin):
5      list_display = ('title','update_date')
6      ordering = ('title',)
7      search_fields = ('title',)
8
9  admin.site.register(Page, PageAdmin)
```

Let's step through the new `PageAdmin` class:

▸ **Line 4.** The `PageAdmin` class inherits from Django's `admin.ModelAdmin` class.

▸ **Line 5.** `list_display` tells Django's admin what model fields to display in the list of pages (i.e., table columns). Here we are setting `list_display` to a tuple containing the `title` and `update_date` fields.

▸ **Line 6.** The `ordering` tuple tells Django's admin which field to use to sort the list. Note, as the tuple only has a single element (singleton), it must have a comma on the end.

▸ **Line 7.** The `search_fields` tuple tells Django's admin which fields should be searched when using the search bar in the model admin. Like `ordering`, `search_fields` is also a singleton, so don't forget the comma!

▸ **Line 9.** We register the `PageAdmin` class with Django's admin.

If you refresh your browser your Pages admin should look like Figure 7-6. You can see that:

1. The list has a new column displaying the Last Updated date for each page;
2. The pages are now listed in alphabetical order; and
3. A new search bar has been added, which allows the user to search for a page using the title field.

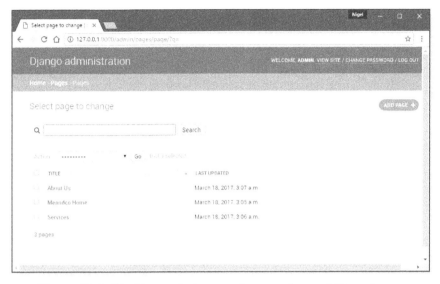

Figure 7-6. *The Page admin now has search capability, the pages are in alphabetical order and a new column displays the Last Updated date.*

Chapter Summary

In this chapter, we created the `Page` model for our `pages` app and populated the database with three pages for our new website.

We also got to use the Django admin for the first time; using the admin to add pages and content. We also got to discover how making a few simple changes to a model can make administering the model much more user-friendly.

In the next chapter, we will take the next step towards a functioning, dynamic website by creating a set of Django templates.

8

Django Templates

In Chapter 6, we created a very simple view to show a message in the browser. This is obviously a long way from a fully functioning modern website—we are missing a *site template.*

Site templates, at their most basic, are HTML files that are displayed by your browser. All websites—from simple, static websites to interactive web applications that work on multiple devices—are built on HTML.

Modern interactive websites are more complex. For example, a modern website will add Cascading Style Sheets (CSS), *semantic markup* and JavaScript in the front end to create the user experience, with a backend like Django supplying the data to show in the template. However, the fundamentals stay the same.

Django's approach to web design is simple—keep Django logic and code separate from design. This means that it's possible for a designer to create a complete front end (HTML, CSS, imagery and user interaction) without ever having to write a single line of Python or Django code.

In this chapter you will learn how to build a simple HTML site template and then add Django *template tags* to create a template capable of displaying data from the database. Before we do this, we need to dive back into your project settings and structure so you can understand where Django looks for templates and how it decides which template to show.

Template Settings

For Django to show your site template, it first must know where to look for the template file(s). This is achieved by the TEMPLATES setting in settings.py. The listing below shows a partial list of template settings:

```
# mfdw_site\settings.py - Default settings.
```

```
1  TEMPLATES = [
2    {
3      'BACKEND': 'django.template.backends.django.
   DjangoTemplates',
4      'DIRS': [],
5      'APP_DIRS': True,
6      'OPTIONS': {
       # ...
```

The important lines in this settings list are lines 4 and 5:

- ▶ **Line 4.** DIRS contains a list of paths to folders containing templates. Paths can be absolute or relative. Default is an empty list.

- ▶ **Line 5.** If APP_DIRS is True, Django will look for a folder named templates in each of your apps. Default is True.

Not all template files will be tied to a particular app. The DIRS setting is useful for linking to templates that exist elsewhere in your project structure. In our project, we will have a site template that is not a part of the pages app, so we need to add a path to DIRS (changes in bold):

```
1  'BACKEND': 'django.template.backends.django.
   DjangoTemplates',
2      'DIRS':
   [os.path.join(BASE_DIR, 'mfdw_site/templates')],
3      'APP_DIRS': True,
```

This looks complicated, but is easy to understand—os.path.join is a Python command to create a file path by joining strings together (concatenating). In this example, we are joining mfdw_site/templates to

our project directory to create the full path to our templates directory, i.e.,
`<your project path>/mfdw_root/mfdw_site/templates`.

Path Names in Django Files

Django uses Linux-style paths in many places—the `settings.py` file is one of them.

This can be a trap for Windows programmers. Make sure you use the forward slash(/) not backslash(\) in file paths in the settings file.

This rule also applies to template paths in Django views which we will see later in this chapter.

Before we move on, we need to create a `templates` directory in our site directory. Once you have created the new directory, your project directory should look like this:

```
\mfdw_project
    \mfdw_root
            \mfdw_site
                    \templates
                # more files ...
```

Static Files

Django treats static files—images, CSS and JavaScript—differently to templates. Django's creators wanted it to be fast and scalable, so right from the beginning Django was designed to make it easy to serve static media from a different server to the one the main Django application was running on.

Django achieves speed and scalability by keeping static media in a different directory to the rest of the application. This directory is defined in the `settings.py` file and is called `static` by default:

```
STATIC_URL = '/static/'
```

This line should be at or near the end of your `settings.py` file. We need to add another setting so that Django can find the static files for our site. Add the following below the `STATIC_URL` setting:

```
STATICFILES_DIRS = [
    os.path.join(BASE_DIR, 'mfdw_site/static'),
]
```

The `STATICFILES_DIRS` list serves the same function for static files as the `DIRS` list does for templates. In this case, we are telling Django to look for static files in the `static` directory in our site root. Now we need to create a `static` folder in our site root. Once you have created the new folder, your project directory will look like this:

```
\mfdw_root
   \mfdw_site
         \static
         \templates
     # more files ...
```

Site Template and Static Files

Now we have configured Django to be able to serve our templates, it's time to create our site template and static files. It's recommended that you create these files yourself, however, the code and media are available for download from the book website[1].

We will be creating four files:

1. **base.html**. The base HTML template for our site
2. **main.css**. CSS styles for our template
3. **logo.jpg**. 30x30 pixels image for the logo
4. **top_banner.png**. 800x200 pixels banner for the site

---

1   https://djangobook.com/mfdw-source

Listings for `base.html` and `main.css` follow. The comment at the top of each listing shows you where to create the file.

Listing 1—base.html

```
# \mfdw_site\templates\base.html
```

```
1  {% load static %}
2  <!doctype html>
3  <html>
4  <head>
5  <meta charset="utf-8">
6  <title>Untitled Document</title>
7  <link href="{% static 'main.css' %}" rel="stylesheet"
   type="text/css">
8  </head>
9  <body>
10 <div id="wrapper">
11   <header id="header">
12     <div id="logo"><img src="{% static 'logo.jpg' %}"
   alt=""/></div>
13     <div id="topbanner"><img src="{% static 'top_
   banner.png' %}" width="800" height="200" alt=""/></div>
14   </header>
15   <aside id="leftsidebar">
16     <nav id="nav">
17     <ul><li>Menu 1</li><li>Menu 2</li><li>Menu 3</li></
   ul>
18     </nav>
19   </aside>
20   <section id="main">
21     <h1>Welcome!</h1>
22     <p>This is the site template</p>
23   </section>
24   <footer id="footer">Copyright &copy; 2017 Meandco Web
   Design</footer>
25 </div>
26 </body>
27 </html>
```

This file is mostly plain HTML5 markup. Note the semantic elements—
`<aside>`, `<section>` and `<footer>`. Semantic elements provide additional
meaning to the browser on how a piece of content should be treated. If you
are not familiar with HTML and want to learn more, you can check out
W3schools[2].

The `base.html` template also includes your first Django template tag—
`{% static %}`. The `static` tag is used to link media in your templates to
the `STATIC_ROOT` of your project. As we are in development and haven't
configured Django for production, `STATIC_ROOT` is the same as your
`STATIC_URL` setting (`/static/`).

▶ **Line 1**. First, we load the `static` tag into the template;

▶ **Lines 7, 12 and 13**. Then, wherever we need to load static media, we
pass the media filename (e.g., `logo.jpg`) to the `static` tag, which will
automatically prepend the static media directory
(e.g., `/static/logo.jpg`).

Listing 2—main.css

```
  # \mfdw_site\static\main.css

1  @charset "utf-8";
2  #header {
3    border-style: none;
4    width: 800px;
5    height: auto;
6  }
7  #wrapper {
8    margin-top: 0px;
9    margin-left: auto;
10   margin-right: auto;
11   background-color: #FFFFFF;
12   width: 800px;
13 }
14 body {
15   background-color: #E0E0E0;
```

```
16    font-family: Gotham, "Helvetica Neue", Helvetica,
   Arial, sans-serif;
17    font-size: 0.9em;
18    text-align: justify;
19    color: #474747;
20 }
21 #footer {
22    text-align: center;
23    font-size: 0.8em;
24    margin-top: 5px;
25    padding-top: 10px;
26    padding-bottom: 10px;
27    background-color: #FFFFFF;
28    border-top: thin solid #BBBBBB;
29    clear: both;
30    color: #969696;
31 }
32 #nav li {
33    padding-top: 10px;
34    padding-bottom: 10px;
35    font-size: 1em;
36    list-style-type: none;
37    border-bottom: thin solid #5F5F5F;
38    color: #4C4C4C;
39    left: 0px;
40    list-style-position: inside;
41    margin-left: -10px;
42 }
43 #nav li a {
44    text-decoration: none;
45 }
46 #leftsidebar {
47    width: 180px;
48    height: 350px;
49    float: left;
50 }
51 #main {
52    width: 560px;
53    float: left;
54    margin-left: 20px;
55    margin-right: 10px;
56    padding-right: 10px;
57 }
```

```
58 #logo {
59   padding: 10px;
60 }
```

This file is standard CSS. If you are not familiar with CSS, you can either enter the code as written and learn more about style sheets as you go, or if you want to learn more now, you can check out W3schools[3].

logo.jpg and top_banner.png

These files can either be downloaded from the book website, or you can create your own. Either way, they both need to be put into the \mfdw_site\static\ folder.

Updating Your View

Now we have the templates and static files in place, we need to update our views.py (changes in bold):

```
  # pages\views.py

1  from django.shortcuts import render
2  # from django.http import HttpResponse
3
4  def index(request):
5      # return HttpResponse("<h1>The Meandco Homepage</
   h1>")
6      return render(request, 'base.html' )
```

For our new view, we have replaced the call to HttpResponse() with a call to render(). I have commented out the original lines (Lines 2 and 5) so that you can more easily see the changes. You don't have to remove the import from django.http, but it's good practice not to import modules that you are no longer using.

---

3   https://www.w3schools.com/css/default.asp

`render()` is a special Django helper function that creates a shortcut for communicating with a web browser. If you remember from Chapter 6, when Django receives a request from a browser, it finds the right view and the view returns a response to the browser.

In the example from Chapter 6, we simply returned some HTML text. However, when we wish to use a template, Django first must load the template, create a *context*—which is basically a dictionary of variables and associated data that is passed back to the browser—and then return a `HttpResponse`.

You can code each of these steps separately in Django, but in the vast majority of cases it's more common (and easier) to use Django's `render()` function which provides a shortcut that provides all three steps in a single function.

When you supply the original request, the template and the context directly to `render()`, it returns the appropriately formatted response without you having to code the intermediate steps.

In our modified `views.py`, we are simply returning the original `request` object from the browser and the name of our site template. We will be getting to the context a bit later in the chapter.

Once you have modified your `views.py` file, save it and fire up the development server. If you navigate to `http://127.0.0.1:8000/`, you should see your shiny new site template (Figure 8-1).

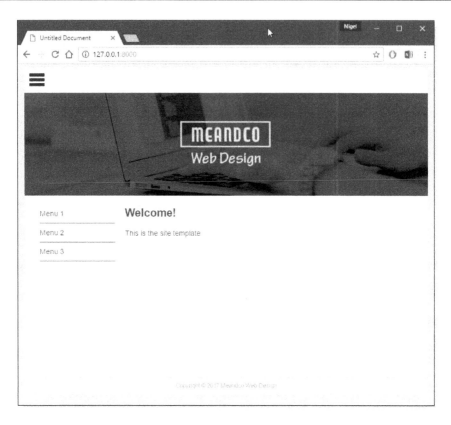

Figure 8-1. The raw HTML template for your Django website.

It Broke!—Django's Error Page

Creating and coding templates for the first time is almost certain to fail as it's difficult to get everything right first go, so it's time for a digression to have a closer look at Django's error page. If you had an error in your template structure or settings, you will get a page that looks like Figure 8-2.

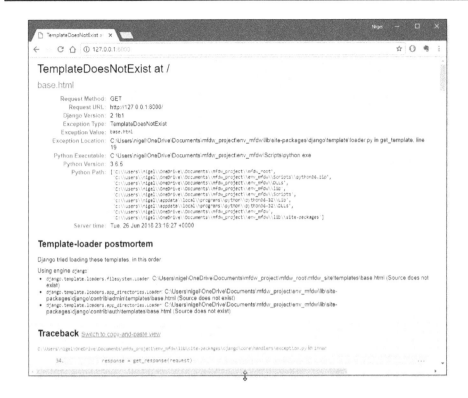

Figure 8-2. *Django's error page provides a huge amount of useful information for when you need to troubleshoot your application.*

Take some time to explore the error page and get to know the various bits of information it gives you. Here are some things to note:

▶ At the top of the page, you get the key information about the exception: the type of exception, any parameters to the exception (the **TemplateDoesNotExist** message in this case), the file in which the exception was raised and the offending line number.

▶ As this is a template error, Django will display a **Template-loader postmortem** to show you where things went wrong.

- Under the key exception information, the page displays the full Python traceback for this exception. This is like the standard traceback you get in Python's command-line interpreter, except it's more interactive.

- For each level (frame) in the traceback, Django displays the name of the file, the function/method name, the line number and the source code of that line. Click the line of source code (in dark gray), and you'll see several lines from before and after the erroneous line, to give you some context on the code that led to the error.

- Click **Local vars** under any frame in the stack to view a table of local variables and their values in that frame at the exact point in the code at which the exception was raised. This debugging information can be a great help.

- Note the **Switch to copy-and-paste view** text under the **Traceback** header. Click the link and the traceback will switch to an alternate version that can be easily copied and pasted. Use this when you want to share your exception traceback with others to get technical support.

- Underneath, the **Share this traceback on a public Web site** button will do this work for you in just one click. Click it to post the traceback to dpaste[4] where you'll get a distinct URL that you can share with other people.

- Next, the **Request information** section includes a wealth of information about the incoming Web request that spawned the error: GET and POST information, cookie values and meta information.

- Below the **Request information** section, the **Settings** section lists all the settings for this particular Django installation.

The Django error page can show a range of different information depending on the type of error. You should consider it your number one troubleshooting tool when your Django app is not working.

It's obvious that much of this information is sensitive. As it exposes the innards of your Python code and Django configuration, a malicious person could use it to attempt to reverse-engineer your web application.

---

4   http://dpaste.com/

For that reason, the Django error page is only shown when a Django project is in debug mode. When we created the project with `startproject`, Django automatically put the site in debug mode. This is OK for now; just know that you must **never** run a production site in debug mode. We will be setting DEBUG to False when we deploy the site to the Internet in Chapter 14.

The Pages Template

Now we have got the site template up and running, we need to create a template for our `pages` app. If you remember the DRY principle from Chapter 3, we don't want to repeat the same information in all our templates, so we want our pages template to inherit from the site template.

Implementing inheritance is easy in Django—you define replaceable blocks in each template so that child templates can replace sections of the parent template with content unique to the child. This is easier to understand with an example, so let's modify base.html (changes in bold):

```
# \mfdw_site\templates\base.html

# ...
<section id="main">
  {% block content %}
    <h1>Welcome!</h1>
    <p>This is the site template</p>
  {% endblock content %}
</section>
# ...
```

The two lines of code we have added are a set of Django *block tags*. A block tag defines a block of template code that can be replaced by any child template that inherits from the template. Block tags have the form:

```
{% block <name> %}{% endblock <name> %}
```

The second `<name>` declaration isn't required, although it's highly recommended, especially if you are using multiple block tags. You can name your block tags anything you like—in our example, we are naming the block tag `content`.

Next, we need to create a template for our `pages` app that inherits from the site template. If you remember from earlier in the chapter, the `APP_DIRS` setting defaults to `True`. This means that Django will search all your apps for a folder named `templates`. Go ahead and create a `templates` folder inside your `pages` app now. We then need to create another folder inside that. This second folder is named `pages` after the app. Your `pages` app folder structure should look like this when you are done:

```
\pages
    \templates
            \pages
```

So, why a second `pages` folder?

What if you have two apps in your project that each have a template named `index.html`? Django uses short circuit logic when searching for templates, so when it goes searching for `templates/index.html`, it will use the first instance it finds and that may not be in the app you wanted!

Adding the inner pages folder is an example of *namespacing* your templates. By adding this folder you can make sure Django retrieves the right template.

Let's go ahead and create our page template—`page.html`:

```
# \pages\templates\pages\page.html

1  {% extends "base.html" %}
2
3  {% block content %}
4  <h1>Welcome!</h1>
5    <p>This is the page template</p>
6  {% endblock content %}
```

Let's have a closer look at this:

▸ **Line 1**. This is where the magic of inheritance comes in. We are telling Django that the page template *extends*, or adds to, the base (site) template.

▸ **Lines 3 to 5**. We are declaring a set of block tags named content. This block will replace the block of the same name in the parent template.

Notice that we have not repeated a single line of code from base.html—we are loading the file with the extends tag and replacing the content block with a new content block.

Now that we have created the page template, we need to modify views.py to show the template (changes in bold):

```
1  from django.shortcuts import render
2
3  def index(request):
4      return render(request, 'pages/page.html' )
```

Only a small change this time—instead of using the site template, we are now using the page template. If you run the development server, your home page should look like Figure 8-3. Notice that it's saying "This is the page template", not "This is the site template". This demonstrates that with only a few lines of code, Django's templates allow you focus on only those things that are different on the page and ignore the parts that are the same.

Cool stuff.

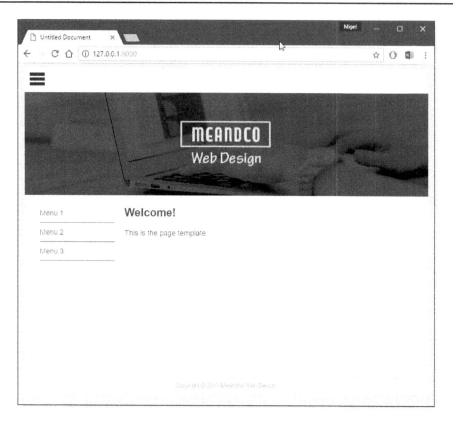

Figure 8-3. *With only a few lines of code, we have now created a page template that inherits all the content from the site template.*

Chapter Summary

We have covered a bit of ground in this chapter, so it's good to step back and have a look at what we have achieved.

First, we learned how Django discovers templates, how it separates static files from your applications to make it easier to scale a Django website and how to add and modify template settings.

Along the way we explored the Django error page and how it can be used to troubleshoot errors in our apps. Finally, we learned how easy it is to turn a basic HTML template into a Django template capable of inheriting common content.

Of course, the templates are still static—the content is hard-coded into the template. In the next chapter we will learn how to show dynamic content in a Django page as well as writing some more complex views.

9

Improving Your View and Adding Navigation

In the last chapter, we created our site template and a page template that inherits from the site template. While our project is finally starting to look like a real website, it's still static—the page template does not display the site content and we still have no site navigation to be able to load different pages on the site.

In this chapter, we will modify the page template to show the selected page content dynamically and turn the placeholder text in the left menu into navigation links to our site pages.

To achieve this outcome, we have four tasks to complete:

1. Modify our URLs to capture a page link;
2. Rewrite our index view to select the correct page and return the content to the template;
3. Modify our templates to show the new content; and
4. Turn the placeholder menu list in the left sidebar into a navigation menu.

Modify Page URLs

If you remember from Chapter 6, we configured our URL dispatcher to load the index view when we navigated to the root URL (http://127.0.0.1:8000/). If we want to open another page, we need to give Django more information.

Common practice is to create a custom URL for each of our pages, for example, /services/ will link to the *Our Services* page. In Chapter 7, when we created the Page model we added a field called permalink. The permalink field contains a text string that our Django application will use to match our URL to the correct page.

For Django to know what page we are requesting, we need to be able to extract the page link from the requested URL. We do this by modifying our urls.py file (changes in bold):

```
# pages\urls.py

1  from django.conf.urls import path
2
3  from . import views
4
5  urlpatterns = [
6      # path('', views.index, name='index'),
7      path('', views.index, {'pagename': ''}, name='home'),
8      path('<str:pagename>', views.index, name='index'),
9  ]
```

I have commented out the original URL pattern (**line 6**), so you can see what has changed. In **line 8**, we are using a *capturing group*. Everything inside the angle brackets will be captured and sent to the view as a parameter (pagename). <str:pagename> is basically saying "capture everything after the domain name and send it to the view as the string parameter pagename". For example, if the URL services/ is passed to this function, the index view is called and the string "services" passed to the view in the pagename parameter.

str: is a *path converter*, which will convert the captured data into a string. Other path converters are available, including int and slug which will convert the captured data to an integer or a text slug respectively. The default is a string, so str: is not technically necessary but, in sticking with the Zen of Python, it's better to be explicit.

Because the path() function is not able to capture an empty string, we must create a special case for the home page, which is exactly what we are doing in **line 7**. When the user navigates to the site root, line 7 will set pagename to an empty string (' ').

Rewriting the View

Once we have changed our URL dispatcher to be able to capture information from the URL, we then modify the index view.

Before we start rewriting the view, let's have a look at how Django works with models to retrieve information from the database. For this exercise, we are going to use the Django interactive shell I introduced in Chapter 5.

From within your virtual environment, run the command:

```
(env_mfdw) ...\mfdw_site> python manage.py shell
```

From Django's interactive shell, enter the following code:

```
1  >>> from pages.models import Page
2  >>> pg = Page.objects.get(permalink='/')
3  >>> pg.title
4  'Meandco Home'
5  >>> pg.update_date
6  datetime.datetime(2017, 3, 18, 3, 5, 47, tzinfo=<UTC>)
7  >>> pg.bodytext
8  '<your page content will show here>'
```

Let's have a closer look at this:

▸ **Line 1.** We import the Page model from our pages app.

▸ **Line 2.** We are retrieving a single page from the database and storing it in the object pg. In this example we are retrieving the home page.

▸ Now that we have a page object, we can access its attributes:

　▷ **Line 3.** Page title

　▷ **Line 5.** Page last update date

　▷ **Line 7.** Page content

Much More to Models!

The models in this book as well as the methods we are using to access them are only just a taste of how powerful Django models are. A deep examination of Django models' capabilities is well beyond the scope of this book. Those wishing to explore further are encouraged to check out the Django Book website[1].

We can now use what we learned in the interactive shell to create a new view:

```
# pages\views.py

1   from django.shortcuts import render
2
3   from . models import Page
4
5   def index(request, pagename):
6       pagename = '/' + pagename
7       pg = Page.objects.get(permalink=pagename)
8       context = {
9           'title': pg.title,
10          'content': pg.bodytext,
11          'last_updated': pg.update_date,
12      }
13      # assert False
14      return render(request, 'pages/page.html', context)
```

Except for the first line, this is all new code, so let's go through it in detail:

▸ **Line 3.** Import the Page model into the view.

▶ **Line 5**. Add the `pagename` parameter to the definition of the `index` view. The string captured by the URL dispatcher will be assigned to `pagename` when the view loads.

▶ **Line 6**. Django removes the slash from the front of our URLs, so we need to prepend a forward slash to `pagename`, otherwise the URL links in our template will be relative to the current page, not relative to the root.

▶ **Line 7**. This is the same code we used to load a page when we were exploring the model in the interactive shell. The `pg` object will contain the page requested by the URL.

▶ **Lines 8 to 12**. We are using our `pg` object to populate a dictionary of items to pass to the template. In Django, this dictionary is called the *context*. The context variables will be used by the template to render dynamic content to the browser.

▶ **Line 13**. Is for testing the view. More on this below.

▶ **Line 14**. `render()` requires a `request` object, the name of the template and the context to be passed to the template. Django will then compile the webpage from the information provided and return a fully rendered HTML page to the browser (`HttpResponse`).

Testing the View

One simple, but very powerful way of testing to make sure the view is passing the right information back to the template is to use Django's error page to examine the output of the view. Django's error page can be triggered by inserting `assert False` into your code. Uncomment line 13 in your code, run the development server and navigate to the root of your website.

When Django's error page shows, scroll to the end of the traceback information (Figure 9-1).

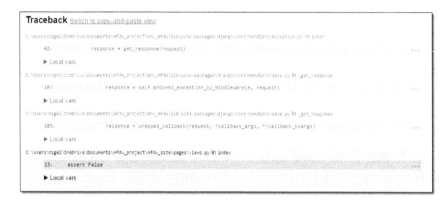

Figure 9-1. Traceback information showing your assert False statement at the end.

If you click on **Local vars,** the frame expands to show the information you are passing to the template. In Figure 9-2, the context dictionary contains the page variables you are passing to the view.

```
▼ Local vars
Variable    Value
context     {'content': '<h1>Welcome to Meandco Web Design!</h1>\r\n'
                        '<p>\r\n'
                        'Vivamus sodales elit sapien, et rhoncus mauris pellentesque non. '
                        'Vestibulum porttitor leo sit amet nisl tincidunt euismod. Fusce a '
                        'sem risus. Maecenas accumsan justo augue, ac maximus augue '
                        'pretium eu. In imperdiet tellus quis enim interdum elementum. '
                        'Nunc fermentum est mauris, sed euismod dolor dictum et. Integer '
                        'pharetra ac elit ultrices consequat. Class aptent taciti sociosqu '
                        'ad litora torquent per conubia nostra, per inceptos himenaeos.\r\n'
                        '</p>\r\n'
                        '<p>\r\n'
                        'Nam quis ante odio. Etiam eget auctor orci. Donec lobortis nisl a '
                        'nunc interdum consectetur. Mauris dictum arcu vel lacinia '
                        'finibus. Curabitur eu leo nisl. Integer vitae posuere mi, eget '
                        'tempus nisl. In hac habitasse platea dictumst. Aliquam rhoncus ac '
                        'nisl sit amet facilisis. Mauris sit amet diam leo. Donec '
                        'dignissim quis dui ut scelerisque. Nunc ullamcorper, odio non '
                        'consequat tristique, nibh sem mattis ex, ut laoreet massa elit '
                        'vel enim.\r\n'
                        '</p>',
            'last_updated': datetime.datetime(2017, 3, 18, 3, 5, 47, tzinfo=<UTC>),
            'title': 'Meandco Home'}
pagename '/'
pg         <Page: Meandco Home>
request    <WSGIRequest: GET '/'>
```

Figure 9-2. The Local vars frame shows all the information you are passing to the view.

This ability to look inside your views is supremely useful. If you get into the habit of using Django's error view in this way, you can dramatically reduce your debugging time when developing more advanced websites.

Now that you have seen how to put the error page to use, it's time to modify the templates (don't forget to comment or delete Line 13 before you move on!).

Modify the Templates

We will take the next bit in stages, so you can see the process broken down into simpler steps. First, we modify the page template to show the page content:

```
# pages\templates\pages\page.html

1   {% extends "base.html" %}
2
3   {% block content %}
4   {{ content }}
5   {% endblock content %}
```

We have only changed one line in this template—we have replaced the placeholder text in Line 4 with a template variable (`{{ content }}`). This variable will contain the page content at runtime.

Save the template and then launch the development server. When you load up the home page, you will notice something is wrong—your nicely formatted HTML is showing in one big ugly block! (Figure 9-3).

This is because Django, by default, auto-escapes any HTML before it's rendered in a template. I have included this as an example of one of the things Django does automatically to protect your website from malicious damage—in this case, where an attacker attempts to inject executable code into your website.

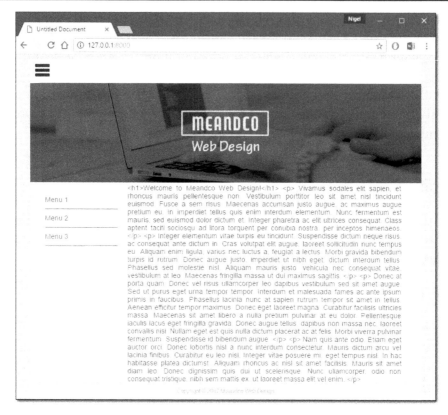

Figure 9-3. Something is not quite right here. The page looks a mess because Django auto-escapes all HTML to protect you from malicious attack.

To prevent Django auto-escaping content you want rendered as HTML, you use the autoescape tag:

```
# pages\templates\pages\page.html
```

```
1  {% extends "base.html" %}
2
3  {% block content %}
4  {% autoescape off %}
5  {{ content }}
6  {% endautoescape %}
7  {% endblock content %}
```

In **lines 4 and 6,** I have surrounded the content variable with an autoescape block so Django doesn't escape any of our page content. If you reload the page, it should now look great! (Figure 9-4).

Figure 9-4. *Remove the automatic escaping from the template and the HTML code now displays correctly.*

Your view should now be working and able to show your site pages. Test it now by trying to navigate to http://127.0.0.1:8000/services and http://127.0.0.1:8000/about. Django should display your Services and About Us pages respectively. If t doesn't, remember that the Django error page gives you a lot of useful information for troubleshooting your site.

Improving the Templates

Our website is looking great, but a couple of things still need to be done to the site and page templates before we create the navigation:

1. Set the page title; and
2. Add the date the page was last updated under the page content.

Page Title

To update the page title for each page, we first need to add a set of block tags to the site template (changes in bold):

```
# mfdw_site\templates\base.html

1  <!doctype html>
2  <html>
3  <head>
4  <meta charset="utf-8">
5  <title>
6      {% block title %}
7          Untitled Document
8      {% endblock title %}
9  </title>
```

This should be straight forward—in **lines 6 and 8** we have entered an opening and closing block tag and named it "title". Now we need to override the new `title` block tag in our page template:

```
# pages\templates\pages\page.html

1  {% extends "base.html" %}
2
3  {% block title %}{{ title }}{% endblock title %}
4
5  {% block content %}
6
7  {% autoescape off %}
8  {{ content }}
```

```
 9  {% endautoescape %}
10
11  <p>
12    Page last updated: {{ last_updated|date:'D d F Y' }}
13  </p>
14
15  {% endblock content %}
```

Line 3 is where the override magic happens—we are replacing the placeholder text in the site template with the `{{ title }}` variable which, at runtime, will contain the title of our page.

I have also added three new lines to this file (**lines 11 to 13**). You should recognize this as a variable tag with additional code. This is an example of applying a *filter* to a template tag.

Django's template language has many filters that do everything from formatting strings to performing minor logical and mathematical operations. In this instance, we are using Django's `date` filter to format the `last_updated` date from our database. We are using a format string that produces a long-form date, e.g. "Tuesday 7th March 2017". There are lots of different format strings for dates; a handy reference is Django's own documentation[2].

Save the files, run the development server and your browser should display the completed home page, with title in the browser tab and nicely formatted date information at the bottom of the page (Figure 9-5).

Well done!

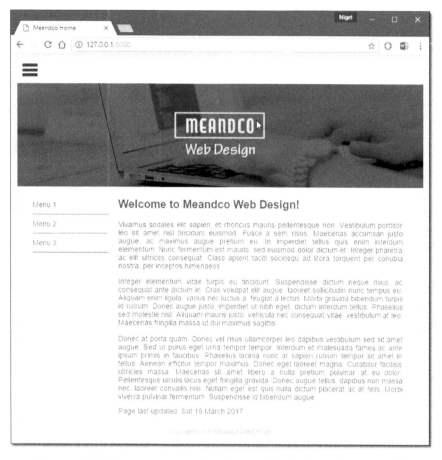

Figure 9-5. Your page template is now displaying the page title and last updated date.

Create a Menu

Now that we can show our page content dynamically, we need a way to navigate our website. We do this with a menu. Menus can get complex in a modern website—with animation and flexible layouts depending on screen size—however, at their most basic, they are simply a list of links to your content.

We will be implementing a menu in the left sidebar of our site, with the title of the page linked to the page content (via the page's permalink). We want a menu entry for each page, so we will be creating an HTML list of the pages of our site, with the page title as the anchor text and the permalink as its URL.

Before we do that, however, let's use the interactive shell to have a look how we retrieve a set of objects (*QuerySet*) from the database. Exit the development server and run the Django interactive shell:

```
(env_mfdw) ...\mfdw_site> python manage.py shell
```

Now follow along by entering the code below and watching the output.

```
1  >>> from pages.models import Page
2  >>> page_list = Page.objects.all()
3  >>> for page in page_list:
4  ...       print(page.permalink, page.title)
5  ...
6  / Meandco Home
7  /services Services
8  /about About Us
9  >>>
```

Let's have a closer look at this code:

▸ **Line 1**. Imports the `Page` model so we can work with our page data.

▸ **Line 2**. The `all()` function returns a list of all `Page` objects in the database. Think of `page_list` as a table where each row is a single page from the database.

▸ **Lines 3 to 5**. We are using a Python `for` loop to iterate over each page (row) in `page_list` and printing out the permalink and title for that page.

▸ **Lines 6 to 8**. The output from the shell. As you can see, for each page in the database, the `for` loop prints out the permalink and the page title.

Moving over to our project, let's use what we have learned to add a list of pages to our view context:

```
# \pages\views.py

  # ...
1 context = {
2       'title': pg.title,
3       'content': pg.bodytext,
4       'last_updated': pg.update_date,
5       'page_list': Page.objects.all(),
6 }
  # ...
```

I have only provided a partial listing of views.py here, but you can clearly see where I have added a variable page_list to the context and populated it with the pages in our database. Now we need to modify the templates to show the new menu.

First the base template:

```
# mfdw_site\templates\base.html

  # ...
1 <nav id="nav">
2   <ul>
3     {% block sidenav %}
4     <li>Menu 1</li><li>Menu 2</li><li>Menu 3</li>
5     {% endblock sidenav %}
6   </ul>
7 </nav>
  # ...
```

This is a partial listing of the base.html file. In **lines 3 and 5** we have entered an opening and closing block tag and named it "sidenav". Now we need to override the new sidenav block tag in our page template:

```
# \pages\templates\pages\page.html

# ... {% endblock title %}
```

```
1   {% block sidenav %}
2       {% for page in page_list %}
3       <li>
4        <a href="{{ page.permalink }}">{{ page.title }}</a>
5       </li>
6       {% endfor %}
7   {% endblock sidenav %}

    {% block content %}
    # ...
```

Again, this is only a partial listing of the file to give you context. Note that it doesn't matter where you put the block in the file, just as long as you don't put it inside another block. I have put it between the `title` and `content` blocks, but you could just as easily put the new block at the end of the file and it still works.

Let's have a look at what this new code does:

▶ **Line 2.** This is Django's template tag for a `for` loop. While the syntax is different, it works exactly the same way as Python's `for` loop.

▶ **Line 4.** The code for our menu item. It's a standard HTML anchor with the page permalink as the URL (`href`) and the page title as the anchor text.

▶ **Lines 3 and 5**. Format the anchor as an HTML list item. Remember, the `<ul></ul>` tags are provided by the `base.html` template, so we don't have to add them here.

▶ **Line 6.** All Django template tags require a closing tag. The `for` tag is no exception.

And that's it—if all has gone to plan, when you start the development server again, you should have a fully functioning website with your three pages displayed correctly and a navigable left menu (Figure 9-6).

Figure 9-6. *The completed page template with fully functioning side menu and page content displayed.*

More Tags and Filters

We have covered only a very small subset of the most common Django template tags and filters in the last couple of chapters. If you want to learn about the more popular template tags and filters, I have provided reference tables in the Appendix starting on page 254. For a full reference, as well as use-cases, see the Django Book website[3].

Page Not Found! Adding a 404

Now that we have our site pages, navigation and templates completed, there is one more thing to take care of—dealing with a page that doesn't exist.

If you navigate to, say, `http://127.0.0.1:8000/notapage`, you will get Django's error page with a **DoesNotExist** error. This is considered a Bad Thing with professional websites, so we need to give the user who entered the incorrect URL a more useful error message.

The correct way to handle a bad URL is with a 404 (Page not found) error message. As with most common web development tasks, Django makes raising a 404 easy with the `get_object_or_404` shortcut. Let's make a small change to our `views.py` to implement this shortcut (changes in bold):

```
# pages\views.py

1  from django.shortcuts import render, get_object_or_404
2
3  # ...
4
5  def index(request, pagename):
6      pagename = '/' + pagename
7      pg = get_object_or_404(Page, permalink=pagename)
8      context = {
9          'title': pg.title,
10         'content': pg.bodytext,
11         'last_updated': pg.update_date,
12         'page_list': Page.objects.all(),
13     }
14     return render(request, 'pages/page.html', context)
```

The magic is in **line 7**—`get_object_or_404` will execute `Page.objects.get(permalink=pagename)` and if no object is returned, it will raise an `Http404` error.

If you try the invalid URL again, you will find that instead of a **Does Not Exist** error, you are now getting **Page not found (404)**. All good so far, we have the right error message at least, but why are we still getting the Django error page?

This is because Django does not show 404 error messages while DEBUG is True. Let's make a couple of changes to our settings.py file:

```
# mfdw_site\settings.py

DEBUG = False

ALLOWED_HOSTS = ['127.0.0.1']
```

Other than setting DEBUG to False, we also have to add the local host address to ALLOWED_HOSTS, otherwise Django's security won't allow us to access the page. If you now try to access the invalid URL, you will get the default 404 error page (Figure 9-7).

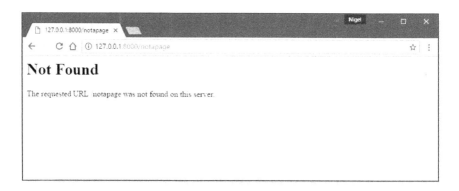

Figure 9-7. A plain and not very useful 404 error page.

As you can see, the default 404 error page is not suitable for a professional website—there is no site template, no navigation and only a very basic message to the user. To render the 404 error page correctly, we have to create a template for it and save the template to our root templates folder. For Django to be able to find it, this file must be called 404.html:

```
# mfdw_site\templates\404.html

{% extends "base.html" %}

{% block title %}Page Not Found{% endblock title %}

{% block sidenav %}
    <li><a href="/">Home</a></li>
{% endblock sidenav %}

{% block content %}
<h1>Aw Crap!</h1>
<p>Not sure where you were going there mate, want to try
again? </p>
<p>Thanks.</p>

{% endblock content %}
```

There's nothing new here—we have just inherited the base template and added some basic navigation and a message to the user.

When DEBUG is set to False, Django will no longer render your static media for you, so the template images and CSS won't display. To test the 404 template, we need to restart the development server with the --insecure option. The --insecure option tells Django that you are still in development mode and to serve the static files. Exit the development server and run it again with:

```
python manage.py runserver --insecure
```

Save the file and navigate to http://127.0.0.1:8000/notapage in your browser. Now when you try to access the invalid URL, you should get a pretty 404 message, rendered with the site template (Figure 9-8).

Creating custom error pages for other HTTP errors (e.g., 500 Server Error) follow the same process.

Don't forget to set DEBUG back to True before moving on to the next chapter.

Figure 9-8. Our custom 404 page not only renders the correct site template, but provides a more helpful message to the user.

Chapter Summary

In this chapter we took a static HTML template and turned it into a fully functioning Django template—complete with a side menu, navigation links and the ability to show page content from your database when one of the menu links is selected. We also covered how to create a custom 404 error page for when someone tries to access the site with an invalid URL.

In the next chapter, we will be adding to your site's capability by adding another essential of modern websites—a contact form.

10
Creating a Contact Form

HTML forms are a core component of modern websites. From Google's simple search box to large, multi-page submissions, HTML forms are the primary means of collecting information from website visitors and users.

The code for a basic HTML form is quite simple, for example:

```
<form>
    <p>First Name: <input type="text" name="firstname"></p>
    <p>Last Name: <input type="text" name="lastname"></p>
    <p><input type="submit" value="submit"></p>
</form>
```

The `<form></form>` HTML tags define the form element and each of the form fields are contained within the form element. In this form, I have defined two text fields and a submit button. In HTML5, there are many other field element types including email fields, date and time fields, checkboxes, radio buttons and more.

You can see that I have rendered the form elements as paragraphs in this example. It's also very common to render forms as an ordered or unordered list or as a table with the fields filling out the rows of the table.

If you were to render this form in a webpage, it would look like Figure 10-1.

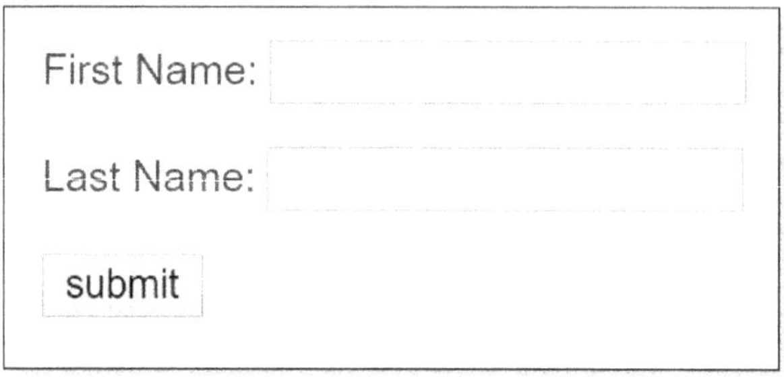

Figure 10-1. *A simple HTML Form*

While creating a basic form is simple, things get much more complicated once you need to use the form in a real-life situation. In an actual website, you must *validate* the data submitted with the form. If the field is required, you must check that the field isn't blank. If the field isn't blank, you then need to check that the data submitted is the valid data type. For example, if you are requesting an email address, you must check that a valid email address is entered.

You must also ensure that your form deals with entered data in a safe way. A common way that hackers target a website is to submit malicious program code via forms to try and hack into the site.

To complicate matters further, website users expect feedback when they haven't filled out a form correctly. So, you must also have some way of displaying errors on the form for the user to correct before allowing them to submit the form.

Creating forms, validating data and providing feedback is a tedious process if you code it all by hand. Django is very flexible in its approach to form creation and management. If you really want to design your forms from scratch like this, Django doesn't do a lot to get in your way.

However, I don't recommend doing this. Unless you have a very special application in mind, Django has many tools and libraries that make form building much simpler. In particular, Django's *form class* offers a very convenient set of class methods that will take care of most of the form processing and validation for you.

With a Form class, you create a special class that looks a lot like a Django model. Form class fields have built-in validation, depending on the field type, as well as an associated HTML widget.

Let's explore the Form class a bit further with the Django interactive shell. From within your virtual environment, run the command:

```
(env_mfdw) ...\mfdw_root> python manage.py shell
```

Once the shell is running, create your SimpleForm class:

```
1  >>> from django import forms
2  >>> class SimpleForm(forms.Form):
3  ...        firstname = forms.CharField(max_length=100)
4  ...        lastname = forms.CharField(max_length=100)
5  ...
6  >>>
```

Let's have a look at what we did here:

▶ **Line 1.** To use the Form class, we need to import the forms module from Django.

▶ **Line 2.** We create our SimpleForm class, which inherits from Django's forms.Form class.

▶ **Lines 3 and 4** are the firstname and lastname fields from our simple HTML form. Notice that the field declarations are almost identical to Django's model field declarations.

This is the first big plus for Django's Form class—you don't have to remember a new syntax for declaring form fields. But it gets better. Let's go back to the shell:

```
1  >>> f = SimpleForm()
2  >>> print(f.as_p())
   <p><label for="id_firstname">Firstname:</label> <input
   type="text" name="firstname" maxlength="100" required
   id="id_firstname"></p>
   <p><label for="id_lastname">Lastname:</label> <input
   type="text" name="lastname" maxlength="100" required
   id="id_lastname"></p>
   >>>
```

Let's see what's happening here:

▶ **Line 1** should be easy enough to follow—we have simply created an instance of the SimpleForm class and named the instance f.

▶ **Line 2** is where the Django magic happens. as_p() is a class method that formats the form as paragraphs. You can see by the output that Django has created your form elements for you without you having to write a single HTML tag!

Django doesn't just output HTML paragraphs—you can also get Django to output HTML for displaying your form as a list or a table. Try these out for yourself:

▶ >>> print(f.as_ul())

▶ >>> print(f.as_table())

You will notice that Django doesn't generate the <form></form> element for you, nor does it generate the <ul></ul> or <table></table> elements or the submit button. This is because they are structural elements on your page, so should remain in the template.

Django's Form class also handles validation for you. Let's go back to the shell to try this out:

```
1  >>> f = SimpleForm({})
2  >>> f.is_valid()
3  False
```

```
4  >>> f.errors
5  {'firstname': ['This field is required.'], 'lastname':
   ['This field is required.']}
```

Reviewing what we did this time:

▸ **Line 1.** We created a new instance of the SimpleForm class and passed an empty dictionary ({}) to the form.

▸ **Line 2.** When Django created the Form class, it made firstname and lastname required by default, so when we run the is_valid() method on the empty form, it returns False.

▸ **Line 4.** Finally, if form validation does fail, Django will create a dictionary of error messages. We can access this dictionary via the errors attribute of the Form class.

One other time-saving feature of the Form class is, when a form doesn't validate, Django re-renders the form with the error messages added automatically. Let's try this out in the shell:

```
>>> print(f.as_p())
<ul class="errorlist"><li>This field is required.</li></
ul>
<p><label for="id_firstname">Firstname:</label> <input
type="text" name="firstname" maxlength="100" required
id="id_firstname"></p>
<ul class="errorlist"><li>This field is required.</li></
ul>
<p><label for="id_lastname">Lastname:</label> <input
type="text" name="lastname" maxlength="100" required
id="id_lastname"></p>
>>>
```

You can see that the errors have been added to the form for you as unordered lists. If you were to render this form in your browser, It would look something like Figure 10-2.

Figure 10-2. *Django's Form class renders the error messages to the form automatically.*

Now that we've had a good look at how Django's `Form` class works, let's create our first form for the website. We are going to start with a simple form that is common to most websites—a contact form.

Creating the Contact Form

To create our `ContactForm` class, we first create a new file called `forms.py`. You could create this file in your site project, but because the contact form is a page on the site, it's more logical to create it inside the pages app:

```
#\pages\forms.py
```

```
1  from django import forms
2
3  class ContactForm(forms.Form):
4      yourname = forms.CharField(max_length=100,
   label='Your Name')
5      email = forms.EmailField(required=False,label='Your
```

```
       e-mail address')
6        subject = forms.CharField(max_length=100)
7        message = forms.CharField(widget=forms.Textarea)
```

This is like the SimpleForm class we were playing with in the shell, with some differences:

▶ **Line 4.** If you don't specify the label attribute, Django uses the field name for the field label. We want the label for the yourname field to be more readable, so we set the label attribute to "Your Name".

▶ **Line 5.** We don't want the email address to be a required field, so we set the required attribute to False, so the person submitting the form can leave the email field blank. We are also changing the default label of the email field to "Your e-mail address".

▶ **Line 7.** The message field must allow the person submitting the form to enter a detailed message, so we are setting the field widget to a Textarea, replacing the default TextInput widget.

Now that we have created our ContactForm class, we have a few tasks to complete to get it to render on our website:

1. Add our form to the list of URLs in our pages app;
2. Add navigation to our site template;
3. Create a template for the contact form; and
4. Create a new view to manage the contact form.

Add URL to Pages App

To show our contact form, first we create a URL for it. To do that, we need to modify our app's urls.py file (changes in bold):

```
# pages\urls.py

1  from django.conf.urls import path
2
```

```
3   from . import views
4
5   urlpatterns = [
6       path('', views.index, {'pagename': ''}, name='home'),
7       path('contact', views.contact, name='contact'),
8       path('<str:pagename>', views.index, name='index'),
9   ]
```

In **line 7** we have added a URLconf that will direct the URL ending in "contact" to the new contact view we will write shortly. Make sure the new URLconf is before the index view in the urlpatterns list. If you put it after the index view URLconf, Django will throw an exception because <str:pagename> will match the contact URL and load the index view instead of the contact view.

Add Navigation to Site Template

The most common place for a link to a website contact form is in the menu, so this is where we are going to add a link for our contact form (changes in bold):

```
# mfdw_site\templates\base.html

# ...
```

```
1   {% block sidenav %}
2       <li>Menu 1</li><li>Menu 2</li><li>Menu 3</li>
3       {% endblock sidenav %}
4       <li><a href="/contact">Contact Us</a></li>
```

We have made one change to the base.html template—in **line 4** we have inserted an additional list item that will be rendered at the end of the other menu items.

Create the Contact Form Template

For our contact form to render, it needs a template. In your
`templates\pages\` directory, create a new file called `contact.html` and
enter the following template code:

```
# pages\templates\pages\contact.html
```

```
1   {% extends "pages/page.html" %}
2
3   {% block title %}Contact Us{% endblock title %}
4
5   {% block content %}
6   <h1>Contact us</h1>
7
8   {% if submitted %}
9       <p class="success">
10          Your message was submitted successfully. Thank
    you.
11      </p>
12
13  {% else %}
14      <form action="" method="post" novalidate>
15      <table>
16          {{ form.as_table }}
17          <tr>
18              <td> </td>
19              <td><input type="submit" value="Submit"></
    td>
20          </tr>
21      </table>
22      {% csrf_token %}
23      </form>
24  {% endif %}
25  {% endblock content %}
```

You will notice that we are extending the page template this time and
replacing the `title` and `content` blocks with new content for our contact
form.

Some other things to note:

▸ **Line 8.** We are using the `{% if %}` template tag for the first time. `submitted` is a boolean value that is passed in from the view. The `{% if %}` / `{% else %}` / `{% endif %}` tags (**lines 8, 13 and 24**) are creating a logical branch that is saying "if the form has been submitted, show the thank you message, otherwise show the blank form."

▸ **Line 14.** Is the beginning of our POST form. This is standard HTML. Note the `novalidate` attribute in the `<form>` tag. When using HTML5 in some of the latest browsers (notably Chrome), form fields will be automatically validated by the browser. As we want Django to handle form validation, the `novalidate` attribute tells the browser not to validate the form.

▸ **Line 16.** This is the line that renders the form fields. The `as_table` method will render the form fields as table rows. Django doesn't render the table tags or the submit button, so we are adding these on **line 15** and **lines 17 to 21**.

▸ **Line 22.** All POST forms that are targeted at internal URLs should use the `{% csrf_token %}` template tag. This is to protect against Cross Site Request Forgeries (CSRF). A full explanation of CSRF is beyond the scope of this book; just rest assured that adding the `{% csrf_token %}` tag is a Good Thing.

Create the Contact Form View

Our final step is to create the new `contact` view. Open your `views.py` file and add the `contact` view code as follows:

```
# pages\views.py

1  from django.shortcuts import render, get_object_or_404
2  from django.http import HttpResponseRedirect
3
4  from . models import Page
```

```
5  from .forms import ContactForm
6
7  # Your index view
8
9  def contact(request):
10     submitted = False
11     if request.method == 'POST':
12         form = ContactForm(request.POST)
13         if form.is_valid():
14             cd = form.cleaned_data
15             # assert False
16             return HttpResponseRedirect('/
   contact?submitted=True')
17     else:
18         form = ContactForm()
19         if 'submitted' in request.GET:
20             submitted = True
21
22     return render(request, 'pages/contact.html',
   {'form': form, 'page_list': Page.objects.all(),
   'submitted': submitted})
```

Let's step through the important bits of this code:

▶ **Lines 2 and 5.** We import the `HttpResponseRedirect` class from `django.http` and the `ContactForm` class from `forms.py`.

▶ **Line 11.** Check if the form was POSTed. If not, skip down to **line 18** and create a blank form.

▶ **Line 13.** Check to see if the form contains valid data. Notice there is no cruft for handling invalid form data. This is what's really cool about the `Form` class. If the form is invalid, the view just needs to drop right through to **line 22** and re-render the form because Django will automatically add the relevant error messages to your form.

▶ **Line 14.** If the form is valid, Django will *normalize* the data and save it to a dictionary accessible via the `cleaned_data` attribute of the `Form` class. In this context, normalizing means changing it to a consistent format. For example, regardless of what entry format you use, Django will always convert a date string to a Python `datetime.date` object.

▶ **Line 15.** We're not doing anything with the submitted form right now, so we put in an assertion error so we can test the form submission with Django's error page.

▶ **Line 16.** Once the form has been submitted successfully, we are using Django's `HttpResponseRedirect` class to redirect back to the contact view. We set the `submitted` variable to True, so instead of rendering the form, the view will render the thank you message.

▶ **Line 22.** Render the template and data back to the view. Note the addition of the `page_list` QuerySet. If you remember from Chapter 9, the page template needs `page_list` to be able to render the menu items.

We're not doing anything with the submitted form data right now, rather I have added an `assert False` to line 15 so we can test that the form is working properly.

Go ahead and uncomment line 15, save the `views.py` file and then navigate to `http://127.0.0.1:8000/contact` to see your new contact form. First, note that there is a link to the contact form in the left menu.

Next, submit the empty form to make sure the form validation is working. You should see the error messages display (Figure 10-3).

Now, fill out the form with valid data and submit again. You should get an assertion error, triggered by the `assert False` statement in the view (line 15). When we wrote our contact form view, we told Django to put the contents of the `cleaned_data` attribute into the variable `cd` (line 14).

With the `assert False` active in our view, we can check the contents of `cd` with the Django error page. Scroll down to the assertion error and open the **Local vars** panel. You should see the `cd` variable containing a dictionary of the complete form submission (Figure 10-4).

Once you have checked the form is working correctly, click on the "Contact Us" link in the menu to take you back to the empty form.

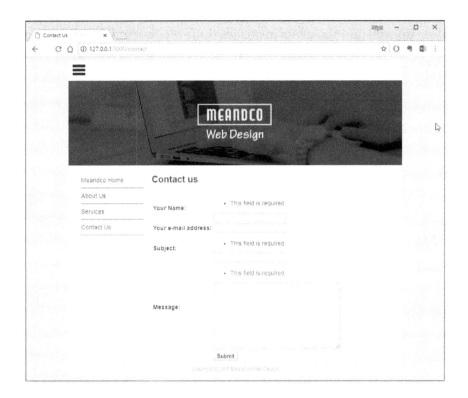

Figure 10-3. *The contact form showing errors for required fields.*

```
D:\OneDrive\Documents\mfdw_project\mfdw_root\pages\views.py in contact
25.            assert False                                              ...
▼ Local vars
Variable   Value
cd         {'email': 'nigel@masteringdjango.com',
            'message': 'the message',
            'subject': 'The subject',
            'yourname': 'Big Nige'}
form       <ContactForm bound=True, valid=True, fields=(yourname;email;subject;message)>
request    <WSGIRequest: POST '/contact'>
submitted  False
```

Figure 10-4. *Using assert False statement allows us to check the contents of the submitted form.*

Our contact form is working great, but it still looks a bit plain—the fields don't line up well and the error messages don't really stand out. Let's make the form prettier with some CSS. Add the following to the end of your main.css file:

```
# main.css

# ...

ul.errorlist {
    margin: 0;
    padding: 0;
}
.errorlist li {
    border: 1px solid red;
    color: red;
    background: rgba(255, 0, 0, 0.15);
    list-style-position: inside;
    display: block;
    font-size: 1.2em;
    margin: 0 0 3px;
    padding: 4px 5px;
    text-align: center;
    border-radius: 3px;
}

input, textarea {
    width: 100%;
    padding: 5px!important;
    -webkit-box-sizing: border-box;
    -moz-box-sizing: border-box;
    box-sizing: border-box;
    border-radius: 3px;
    border-style: solid;
    border-width: 1px;
    border-color: rgb(169,169,169)
}

input {
    height: 30px;
}
.success {
```

```
    background-color: rgba(0, 128, 0, 0.15);
    padding: 10px;
    text-align: center;
    color: green;
    border: 1px solid green;
    border-radius: 3px;
}
```

Once you have saved the changes to your CSS file, refresh the browser and submit the empty form. Not only should your form be better laid out, but showing pretty error messages too (Figure 10-5).

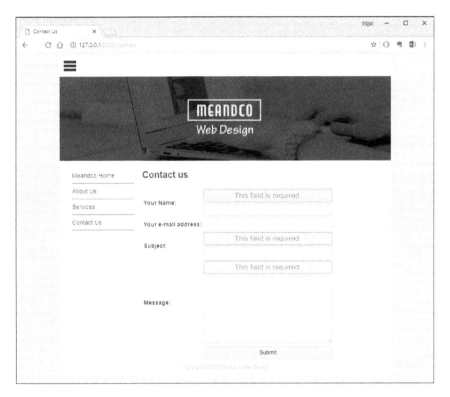

Figure 10-5. *Adding some CSS changes our rather plain contact form into something to be proud of.*

Emailing the Form Data

Our contact form is working well and looking good, but it's not much use right now because we aren't doing anything with the form data.

As this is a contact form, the most common way to deal with form submissions is to email them to a site administrator or some other contact person within the organization.

Setting up an email server to test emails in development can be a real pain. Luckily, this is another problem for which the Django developers have provided a handy solution. Django provides a number of email backends, including a few specifically designed for use during development.

We will be using the `console` backend. This backend is particularly useful in development as it doesn't require you to set up an email server while you are developing a Django application. The `console` backend sends email output to the terminal (console). You can check this in your terminal window after you submit your form.

There are other email back ends for testing—`filebased`, `locmem` and `dummy`, which send your emails to a file on your local system, save it in an attribute in memory or send to a dummy back end respectively.

You can find more information in the Django documentation under Email Backends[1].

So, let's go ahead and modify the contact view to send emails (changes in bold):

```
# pages\views.py

1  from django.shortcuts import render, get_object_or_404
2  from django.http import HttpResponseRedirect
3  from django.core.mail import send_mail, get_connection
4
```

1   https://docs.djangoproject.com/en/2.1/topics/email/#topic-email-backends

```
 5  from . models import Page
 6  from .forms import ContactForm
 7
 8  # Your index view
 9
10  def contact(request):
11      submitted = False
12      if request.method == 'POST':
13          form = ContactForm(request.POST)
14          if form.is_valid():
15              cd = form.cleaned_data
16              # assert False
17              con = get_connection('django.core.mail.
    backends.console.EmailBackend')
18              send_mail(
19                  cd['subject'],
20                  cd['message'],
21                  cd.get('email', 'noreply@example.com'),
22                  ['siteowner@example.com'],
23                  connection=con
24              )
25              return HttpResponseRedirect('/
    contact?submitted=True')
26      else:
27          form = ContactForm()
28          if 'submitted' in request.GET:
29              submitted = True
30
31      return render(request, 'pages/contact.html',
    {'form': form, 'page_list': Page.objects.all(),
    'submitted': submitted})
```

Let's have a look at the changes we've made:

▶ **Line 3.** Import the send_mail and get_connection functions from django.core.mail.

▶ **Line 16.** Comment out the assert False statement. if we don't do this, we will keep getting the Django error page.

▶ **Lines 18 to 24.** Use the send_mail function to send the email.

This is all you need to send an email in Django. If this were a real website, all you would need for production is to change the backend and add your mailserver settings to settings.py.

Test the view by filling out the form and submitting. If you look in the console window (PowerShell or command prompt) you will see that the view sent the coded email straight to the console. For example, when I submitted the form, this was what Django output to PowerShell (I've shortened some of the longer lines):

```
Content-Type: text/plain; charset="utf-8"
MIME-Version: 1.0
Content-Transfer-Encoding: 7bit
Subject: The subject
From: nigel@masteringdjango.com
To: siteowner@example.com
Date: Fri, 17 Aug 2018 01:48:42 -0000
Message-ID: <15344...6882689@DESKTOP-INQV0G1.home>

the message
-----------------------------------------------------------
```

Now that the form is complete, you will also note that when you enter valid data and submit the form, the contact view will redirect to the contact page with "submitted=True" as a GET parameter—http://127.0.0.1:8000/contact?submitted=True.

With submitted set to True, the contact.html template will execute the first {% if %} block and render the success message instead of the form (Figure 10-6).

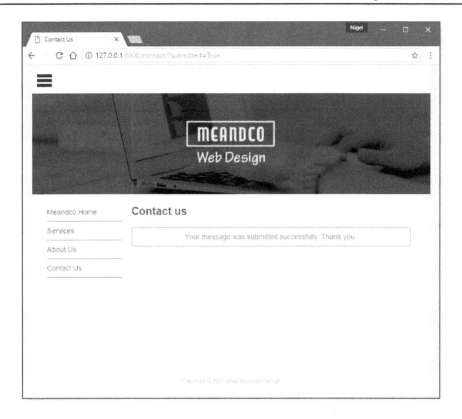

Figure 10-6. *Once a valid form has been submitted, the thank you message is displayed instead of the form.*

Chapter Summary

In this chapter we learned about Django's Form class by creating a simple contact form for our site. We first created the Form class and then the view and template necessary to display the form.

In the next chapter, we are going to take what we have learned and build a more complex model form for collecting data from our website users.

11

Building a More Complex Form

The contact form we built in the last chapter is a common, but very simple use of a website form. Another common use for forms is to collect information from the user and save that information in the database. Examples include entering your personal information for a membership application, your name and address details for a sales order and filling out a survey.

Using forms for collecting and saving data from users is so common that Django has a special form class to make creating forms from Django models much easier—*model forms*.

With model forms, you create a Django model and then create a form that inherits from Django's `ModelForm` class. As always, the devil is in the detail, so in this chapter we're going to build a new Django app from scratch; adding a new model and model form to demonstrate how it all works.

Meandco, being a web design company, needs a way for new and existing customers to submit a request for quotation. Once the quote request has been submitted, it needs to be saved to the database so the staff at Meandco can review the customer's requirements and get back to the customer with a quote.

Remember that Django best-practice says that each Django app should do one thing only. To achieve the result we want, we must first go through the process of creating a new Django app.

The process is the same as we followed to create the `pages` app:

1.   Create the new `quotes` app;
2.   Create the `Quote` model and add it to the database; and
3.   Add the `Quote` model to the Django admin. This time, we are also going to tweak the admin user interface to make managing the quote data easier.

Once the new app is set up and running, we can then create the model form, view and template so website users can submit a request for quotation.

Create the Quotes App

As I mentioned in the introduction, a Django app should only do one thing whenever possible. Collecting and managing quote requests from our site users is a very different application to showing site pages, so we need to create a new Django app for quotes. Make sure your virtual environment is running, then run the following command from inside the `\mfdw_root` directory:

```
(env_mfdw).../mfdw_root> python manage.py startapp quotes
```

If you executed this command correctly, you will now have a new app (quotes) at the same level as the `pages` app in your project directory. While you are at it, add an `\uploads` folder at the same level as your quotes app. You will need this folder to store uploaded quote files:

```
\mfdw_root
    \mfdw_site
    \pages
    \quotes
    \uploads # add this folder while you are here.
```

To register the app with our Django project, we need to add the quotes app configuration to our INSTALLED_APPS list in our settings file (changes in bold):

```
# \mfdw_site\settings.py

INSTALLED_APPS = [
    'pages.apps.PagesConfig',
    'quotes.apps.QuotesConfig',
    'django.contrib.admin',

    # more settings ...
```

Create the Quote Model

When Django created the quotes app for you, it also created a new models.py file for the app. Open this new file (not models.py from your pages app) and enter the following:

```
# mfdw_root\quotes\models.py

1  from django.db import models
2  from django.contrib.auth.models import User
3
4  STATUS_CHOICES = (
5      ('NEW', 'New Site'),
6      ('EX', 'Existing Site'),
7  )
8
9  PRIORITY_CHOICES = (
10     ('U', 'Urgent - 1 week or less'),
11     ('N', 'Normal - 2 to 4 weeks'),
12     ('L', 'Low - Still Researching'),
13 )
14
15 class Quote(models.Model):
16     name = models.CharField(max_length=100)
17     position = models.CharField(max_length=60,
   blank=True)
```

```
18       company = models.CharField(max_length=60,
   blank=True)
19       address = models.CharField(max_length=200,
   blank=True)
20       phone = models.CharField(max_length=30, blank=True)
21       email = models.EmailField()
22       web = models.URLField(blank=True)
23       description = models.TextField()
24       sitestatus = models.CharField(max_length=20,
   choices=STATUS_CHOICES)
25       priority = models.CharField(max_length=40,
   choices=PRIORITY_CHOICES)
26       jobfile = models.FileField(upload_to='uploads/',
   blank=True)
27       submitted = models.DateField(auto_now_add=True)
28       quotedate = models.DateField(blank=True, null=True)
29       quoteprice = models.DecimalField(decimal_places=2,
   max_digits=7, blank=True, default=0)
30       username = models.ForeignKey(User, blank=True,
   null=True, on_delete=models.CASCADE)
31
32       def __str__(self):
33           return str(self.id)
```

This is a much bigger model than our Page model, but the fundamentals are the same, so don't be daunted. Let's step through some of the more important parts:

▶ **Line 2.** We will be accessing the user database to link a user to the quote, so we need to import the User class from django.contrib.auth.models. More on this later.

▶ **Lines 4 to 7.** STATUS_CHOICES is a tuple of two-element tuples (two-tuples) which will translate into a drop-down list of options on the model form in both the admin and on the website. This could also be entered as a list of tuples, however, best-practice is to use tuples as they are immutable (can't be changed). The first element in the tuple is the value that will be saved to the database, the second element is the human-readable name.

▶ **Lines 9 to 13.** PRIORITY_CHOICES is the same as STATUS_CHOICES; it will be translated to a list of options in forms.

▶ **Line 24.** The `sitestatus` field has an additional `choices` attribute. When you set the `choices` attribute, Django will replace the standard `TextInput` widget with the `Select` widget. The `Select` widget displays a drop-down list populated with the contents of the `choices` attribute, i.e., `STATUS_CHOICES`.

▶ **Line 25.** The `priority` field also sets the `choices` attribute. In this case, the drop-down list in the `Select` widget is provided by `PRIORITY_CHOICES`.

▶ **Line 26.** We are using a `FileField` for the first time in a model. We provide the `upload_to` attribute so Django knows where to put uploaded files.

▶ **Line 27.** We set the `auto_now_add` attribute to `True`. This will automatically save the current date and time in the `submitted` field.

▶ **Line 28.** Django never sets a date field to blank, so to allow the `quotedate` field to be empty, we also need to set the `null` attribute to `True` to allow Django to save a Null entry when `quotedate` is empty.

▶ **Line 30.** We have added a foreign key link to the `User` model. Empty values are not allowed for foreign keys, so we set the `null` attribute to `True`. The `on_delete` attribute is required—if you don't set it, Django will throw an error. We set `on_delete` to `CASCADE` which will delete all related entries in other tables. The function of this link will become apparent in a later chapter.

Now that we have created the model, let's make sure everything has been entered correctly with the `check` management command:

```
(env_mfdw) C:\...\mfdw_root> python manage.py check
```

If the model was entered correctly, you should see something like this in your terminal:

```
System check identified no issues (0 silenced).
```

Next, we need to create and run the migrations. Here is the terminal listing for you to check against your output:

```
(env_mfdw) ... \mfdw_root> python manage.py makemigrations
Migrations for 'quotes':
  quotes\migrations\0001_initial.py
    - Create model Quote

(env_mfdw) C:\...\mfdw_root> python manage.py migrate
Operations to perform:
  Apply all migrations: admin, auth, contenttypes, pages,
quotes, sessions
Running migrations:
  Applying quotes.0001_initial... OK
```

And that's it for the Quote model. Now we need to add it to the admin so we can manage incoming quote requests.

Add Quote Model to the Django Admin

To be able to manage incoming quotes, we need to add the Quote model to the admin. This is straight forward; let's start with registering a simple admin class like we did in Chapter 7:

```
# \quotes\admin.py

from django.contrib import admin
from .models import Quote

admin.site.register(Quote)
```

I won't go over this because it should be familiar by now. The purpose of this code is to make sure the admin is working OK with your model. Fire up the development server and navigate to http://127.0.0.1:8000/admin/ and try to add a new quote.

If all has worked to plan, you should see a blank form with your quote fields ready to fill out. The problem here is apparent—the form is huge! So big, in fact, I haven't put a screenshot in the book because it won't fit on the page!

So how do we make this form more manageable? Let's build upon what we learned in Chapter 7 and improve the management interface for the Quote model (changes in bold):

```
# \quotes\admin.py

1  from django.contrib import admin
2  from .models import Quote
3
4  class QuoteAdmin(admin.ModelAdmin):
5      list_display = ('id', 'name', 'company',
   'submitted', 'quotedate', 'quoteprice')
6      list_filter = ('submitted', 'quotedate')
7      readonly_fields = ('submitted',)
8      fieldsets = (
9          (None, {
10             'fields': ('name', 'email', 'description')
11         }),
12         ('Contact Information', {
13             'classes': ('collapse',),
14             'fields': ('position', 'company',
   'address', 'phone', 'web')
15         }),
16         ('Job Information', {
17             'classes': ('collapse',),
18             'fields': ('sitestatus', 'priority',
   'jobfile', 'submitted')
19         }),
20         ('Quote Admin', {
21             'classes': ('collapse',),
22             'fields': ('quotedate', 'quoteprice',
   'username')
23         }),
24     )
25
26 admin.site.register(Quote, QuoteAdmin)
```

Refresh the admin after these changes, and click the **Add quote** link. The form should look like Figure 11-1. Much neater.

Figure 11-1. *The quote form is now much easier to manage with fields grouped into collapsible panels.*

There are a few significant elements to the `QuoteAdmin` class, so we will work through them with some examples and a few screenshots to illustrate what's going on.

Enter a couple of test quotes—you only need to fill out the fields where the field name is in bold. Don't forget to expand the **Contact Information** and **Job Information** group to enter additional quote data. Don't worry about the **Quote Admin** group at this stage.

Once you have added a couple of quotes, the quote listings should look like Figure 11-2. From this screenshot we can see what additional formatting and model management tweaks our QuoteAdmin class has provided—list_display (**line 5**) governs what columns are displayed in the list and list_filter (**line 6**) tells the Django admin what fields to provide filters for (filters are on the right of screen).

Filtering becomes useful when the number of records in your database gets larger. For example, you could filter the quote list to show only the quotes that have been submitted this month.

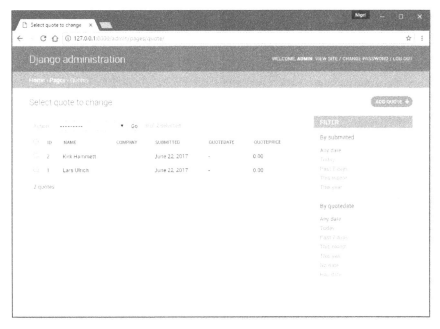

Figure 11-2. The fully formatted quote list summarizes relevant information in columns and provides convenient data filters for quotes.

The collapsible grouping of fields in the admin form is configured with the fieldsets option (**Line 8**) in our QuoteAdmin class. The fieldsets option controls the layout of the add and edit pages in the admin. It's a set of two-tuples (`<name>`, `<field_options>`), one two-tuple for each group of form fields on the form. The order of the two-tuples governs the order in which the field groups are shown in each section on the admin page.

name is the name given to the group. If name is set to None, then no group title will be shown. field_options is a dictionary of options for the group of fields in each section of the form.

Let's see how that works in practice. Here is our first fieldset:

```
(None, {
        'fields': ('name', 'email', 'description')
    }),
```

This fieldset will display name, email and description as the first three fields on the admin form, with no section title (Figure 11-3).

Figure 11-3. The None field name causes the fields in the group to be shown without a group title.

The following three fieldsets group the remaining fields into three sections:

1. Contact Information;
2. Job Information; and
3. Quote Admin.

Each of these fieldsets has an additional `classes` option (**lines 13, 17 and 21**) which applies the `collapse` class to the fieldset. `collapse` is a special built-in class that uses JavaScript to apply an accordion to a set of fields. You can see the effect of this class in Figure 11-4—each of the last three fieldsets appear collapsed when the form is first shown. To expand the section, you just click on the (Show) link.

Figure 11-4. The fieldset options group the form fields, and the "collapse" class puts them in a handy JavaScript collapsible panel.

One last thing before we move on—open up the **Job Information** group and you will notice the **Submitted** field is not editable (Figure 11-5).

Figure 11-5. The Submitted field shown as a read-only field in the admin form.

Because this is a time-stamped field (created by setting `auto_now_add=True` on the model), it can't be edited in the admin. If we tried to show it in the form, we would get an error. So, we set the `readonly_fields` option (**line 7**) on the admin model to include the `submitted` field so it can be shown in the form as read-only.

Now that our quotes app is up and running and the model admin sorted, it's time to create the model form and associated view and template that will allow us to display the form on the website and collect request for quote submissions from Meandco customers.

The process is as follows:

1. Create the `QuoteForm` model form for collecting the quote request information from the user;

2. Add a new view to manage the form;

3. Create the form template; and

4. Add our new view and form to our `urls.py` file and update the site template to link to the quote form.

Create the Quote Form

This is where the power of Django's `ModelForm` class really shines—creating a form for the model is an almost trivial task. Create a new `forms.py` file in your quotes app and enter the following code:

```
# \quotes\forms.py

1   from django import forms
2   from django.forms import ModelForm
3   from .models import Quote
4
5   class QuoteForm(ModelForm):
6       required_css_class = 'required'
7       class Meta:
8           model = Quote
9           fields = [
10              'name', 'position', 'company', 'address',
11              'phone', 'email', 'web', 'description',
12              'sitestatus', 'priority', 'jobfile'
13          ]
```

That's it—a few lines of code is all Django needs to create a form for your model that will display all the necessary HTML on the page, validate your form fields and pass form data to your view. There are some things to note, however, so let's look at those now:

▶ **Line 2.** We import the `ModelForm` class, which will do all the heavy lifting for us.

▶ **Line 5.** Our `QuoteForm` class inherits from `ModelForm`.

▶ **Line 6.** This is a handy `ModelForm` class option that adds a CSS class to our required fields. We will use this class to add an asterisk (*) to the required fields in the form template.

▶ **Line 7.** The `ModelForm` class has an internal `class Meta` which we use to pass in the metadata options the `ModelForm` class needs to render our form:

  ▷ **Line 8.** The model on which to base our form; and

  ▷ **Line 9.** The model fields to render on the form.

Add the Quote View

The quote view also builds on what we have learned previously in the book. We are going to call the new view `quote_req`, so let's go ahead and add the view code to the `views.py` file in our `quotes` app:

```
# \quotes\views.py

1  from django.shortcuts import render
2  from django.http import HttpResponseRedirect
3
4  from .models import Quote
5  from .forms import QuoteForm
6  from pages.models import Page
7
8  def quote_req(request):
9      submitted = False
10     if request.method == 'POST':
11         form = QuoteForm(request.POST, request.FILES)
12         if form.is_valid():
13             form.save()
14             return HttpResponseRedirect('/
```

```
       quote/?submitted=True')
15     else:
16         form = QuoteForm()
17         if 'submitted' in request.GET:
18             submitted = True
19
20     return render(request, 'quotes/quote.html',
   {'form': form, 'page_list': Page.objects.all(),
   'submitted': submitted})
```

This view is functionally identical to the view for our contact form, except we have removed the code for emailing the form data, and replaced it with the form.save() method to save the form data to our database (**line 13**).

One other important change to note—in **line 11** we have added request.FILES to the arguments passed to the QuoteForm class. This is so we can retrieve file upload information from the response.

Create the Quote Form Template

Now it's time to create the template for our form. We will inherit from the site's base template, so the form will be very similar to the contact form template. There's one major difference—the HTML form must be a multi-part form so that we are able to upload a file with the form.

First, create a new \templates folder in your quotes app and add another folder inside that (called \quotes) and add the following code:

```
# \quotes\templates\quotes\quote.html

1  {% extends "base.html" %}
2
3  {% block title %}Quote Request{% endblock title %}
4
5  {% block sidenav %}
6      {% for page in page_list %}
7          <li><a href="{{ page.permalink }}">{{ page.
   title }}</a></li>
8      {% endfor %}
9  {% endblock sidenav %}
```

```
10
11  {% block content %}
12  <h1>Quote Request</h1>
13
14  {% if submitted %}
15      <p class="success">
16          Your quote was submitted successfully. Thank
    you.
17      </p>
18
19  {% else %}
20      <form action="" enctype="multipart/form-data"
    method="post" novalidate>
21      <table>
22          {{ form.as_table }}
23          <tr>
24              <td> </td>
25              <td><input type="submit" value="Submit"></
    td>
26          </tr>
27      </table>
28      {% csrf_token %}
29      </form>
30  {% endif %}
31  {% endblock content %}
```

This code should be straight forward, so I won't go over it in detail. The
only change from what you have seen before is **line 20**, where we set the
enctype of the form to `multipart/form-data` to handle the file upload.

While we are working on the form template, we need to add a little tweak
to the `main.css` file so that our required field labels will have an asterisk
appended to the label:

```
# add to end of \static\main.css

.required label:after {
    content: "*";
}
```

Link the Quote Form

Now we have got the model, the admin and the form sorted, we must add URLconfs to link the form from our site urls.py, create a urls.py file for our quotes app and add a link to the base template (changes in bold):

```python
# \mfdw_site\urls.py

from django.contrib import admin
from django.urls import include, path

urlpatterns = [
    path('admin/', admin.site.urls),
    path('quote/', include('quotes.urls')),
    path('', include('pages.urls')),
]

# \quotes\urls.py (new file)

from django.urls import path

from . import views

urlpatterns = [
    path('', views.quote_req, name='quote-request'),
]

# mfdw_site\templates\base.html

# ...

{% block sidenav %}
    <li>Menu 1</li><li>Menu 2</li><li>Menu 3</li>
    {% endblock sidenav %}
    <li><a href="/contact">Contact Us</a></li>
    <li><a href="/quote/">Get a Quote</a></li>
```

Pay close attention, we're working with three different files here—the file name and path is at the top of each listing. I have grouped them together because they are simple, but related, changes to the linking in your app.

Finished!

Phew! That was a lot to get through, but now if you navigate to `http://127.0.0.1:8000/quote/`, you should see a page just like Figure 11-6.

You will notice that a new menu item has also been added to the left menu and that you can navigate easily to the other site pages. Enter a few quotes now, as we will be using them in the next chapter. Don't forget to attach some files to test the file upload capability of your form.

Figure 11-6. *Our completed form, ready for current and new customers to submit a quote request.*

In the Event of an Emergency...

As this is the most complicated exercise we have completed so far, it's likely that this didn't work first go for you. Don't be too concerned—it crashed something like 30 times before I got it right; so don't think you are alone!

Just remember that Django's error page has a wealth of information that will help you sort out what is going wrong. Use it to find the error and check your code against the code in the book, fix the error and move on to the next. This is exactly how the pros do it—so not something to worry about; it's part of the process.

Chapter Summary

In this chapter we created a quote request form. We implemented a much more complex form than the contact form from the last chapter and created a tool for collecting information from a website user and storing it in our database.

We learned how to manage a more complex model in the admin and how to use Django's `ModelForm` class to make creating forms for models a breeze. We finished with creating a template and the necessary links to integrate our quote form into the rest of the website.

In the next chapter, we will explore the power of Django's generic views to create list and detail pages for quote requests from our site users.

12

Django's Generic Views

At the fundamental level, a view is a piece of code that accepts a request and returns a response. While all the views we have created so far have been *function-based* views, Django also has *class-based* views.

When Django was first created, there were only function-based views included with Django. As Django grew it was clear that, while function-based views covered simple cases well, extending and customizing them proved difficult.

Class-based views provide an alternative way for implementing views in Django. Note the use of the word alternative—there is nothing in Django stopping you from using function-based views if you want to.

Django's class-based views are not designed to replace function-based views, but to provide the advantages of using classes in views. Advantages of class-based views include:

▶ Ability to implement HTTP methods like GET and POST as class methods, instead of conditional branching in code;

▶ Extending and adding functionality to basic classes with inheritance;

▶ Allowing the use of *mixins* and other object-oriented techniques; and

▶ Abstracting common idioms and patterns into generic views to make view development easier for common cases.

It's this last point we will be covering in this chapter. In keeping with the common theme of aiding rapid development, Django's developers have created several class-based *generic views* to aid in implementing common cases.

All of Django's generic views inherit from the View class. In practice, you won't often work with the View class directly. More often, you will work with the generic views that inherit from it.

There are two base views that inherit from the View class—TemplateView and RedirectView. TemplateView simply returns the named template with a context containing whatever was captured from the URL and RedirectView redirects to a given URL.

These base views provide most of the functionality needed to implement class-based views in Django and can either be inherited or used on their own. For example:

```
1      from django.views.generic.base import TemplateView
2
3      urlpatterns = [
4          path('testpage', TemplateView.as_
   view(template_name='pages/page.html')),
5          # ...
```

You can see in **line 4**, the URL testpage creates a TemplateView class instance with the name of the template passed in as a parameter. If you were to add the above code to your site urls.py to test this (and I encourage you to do so), you will find by navigating to http://127.0.0.1:8000/testpage your website app will show a blank page template—all without you having to add a single line of view code. Cool, huh?

In addition to the base views, Django provides several generic views to make view development easier. Most commonly used are the generic display views—DetailView and ListView—that we will be learning about in this chapter.

There are also generic editing views and generic date views provided by Django that are not covered in this book. If you do want to dig deeper into all the generic views provided by Django, see the documentation.[1]

Viewing Records with ListView

The first generic view we will be implementing on our website is ListView. Using the ListView class is very straight forward—first, let's create a new class in our views.py:

```
# \quotes\views.py

1   from django.shortcuts import render
2   from django.http import HttpResponseRedirect
3   from django.views.generic.list import ListView
4
5   from .models import Quote
6   from .forms import QuoteForm
7   from pages.models import Page
8
9   class QuoteList(ListView):
10      model = Quote
11      context_object_name = 'all_quotes'
12
13  def quote_req(request):
14  # ...
```

As you can see, the amount of code necessary to implement the generic view is minimal. Apart from **line 3**, where we import the ListView class, we only need another three lines of code to create the class:

▶ **Line 9.** The class declaration;

▶ **Line 10.** Tells Django which model to use for the view; and

▶ **Line 11.** Tells Django what to name the QuerySet that is passed to the template.

---

1   https://docs.djangoproject.com/en/2.1/ref/class-based-views/

Line 11 is not necessary for the class to function, however, without it the QuerySet passed to the template will be named "object_list". This is not very user-friendly for template designers and can lead to confusion when multiple generic views are used, so best to name it something meaningful.

Next, we need to update the URLs in our `quotes` app to include the new list view (changes in bold):

```
# \quotes\urls.py

1  from django.conf.urls import url
2
3  from . import views
4  from .views import QuoteList
5
6  urlpatterns = [
7      path('', views.quote_req, name='quote-request'),
8      path('show', QuoteList.as_view(), name='show-quotes')
9  ]
```

This should be familiar by now. First, we include the `QuoteList` view (**line 4**), and then we create a URLconf in the app that loads the `QuoteList` generic view (**line 8**).

To test that everything is OK so far, fire up the development server and navigate to `http://127.0.0.1:8000/quote/show`. If your code is working correctly, Django should show a **TemplateDoesNotExist** error.

Take note of the **Exception Value:** field at the top of the error page. It should be set to `quotes/quote_list.html`.

I got you to run the server and trigger this error to illustrate a point. To make development faster and easier, Django's generic views make some assumptions. One of them is that the name of the template for the generic view is going to be the model name with "_list.html" appended. In the case of our quote list view, the template name is assumed to be `quote_list.html`.

Like most things in Django, this default can be overridden, but without good reason, it's best to stick with the default.

Now that we have tested the view and URLs, let's go ahead and create the template:

```
# \quotes\templates\quotes\quote_list.html

1   {% extends "quotes/quote.html" %}
2
3   {% block title %}All Quotes{% endblock title %}
4
5   {% block content %}
6   <h1>All Quotes</h1>
7
8   <ul>
9       {% for quote in all_quotes %}
10          <li>{{ quote.name }}</li>
11      {% endfor %}
12  </ul>
13
14  {% endblock content %}
```

There is nothing new here—we are simply creating a template that inherits from quote.html and rendering the name of the person requesting the quote in an HTML list.

Once you have saved the template, navigate to http://127.0.0.1:8000/quote/show and your webpage should look like Figure 12-1.

While it's not particularly useful, it's clear our template and new view are working, so now we will add fields and formatting to the template so that our list of quotes looks like something we can be proud of.

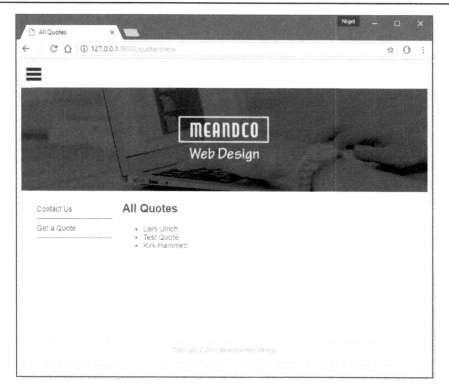

Figure 12-1. While it isn't much use right now, our test demonstrates that the view is working.

You're Agile Now!

It might not seem like it, but this iterative approach to development—getting a simple piece of code working and then building on it to create the outcome you want—is the basis of agile software development.

While there are many different methodologies built upon this concept (Scrum, for example), they all share the same basic principle.

If you get into the habit of asking yourself "what is the minimum amount of code I need to write to demonstrate this works?" You are well on your way to becoming a professional programmer.

Improving the Quote List Template

Adding fields and formatting to our template to show a more useful quote list is quite easy and uses code and techniques that you have already learned earlier in the book.

As we are displaying tabular information, we will be replacing the simple list we used to test the template with a table and rendering each quote record as a row in the table. While we are at it, I will introduce you to a few new Django template tags and filters as we build the template.

Go ahead now and replace the content block in your template with the following:

```
# \quotes\templates\quotes\quote_list.html

# ...

1  {% block content %}
2  <h1>All Quotes</h1>
3
4  <table style="border-collapse:collapse">
5      <tr class="quotehdr"><th>ID</th><th>Client Name
   </th>
6          <th>Company</th><th>Submitted</th>
7          <th>Quoted</th><th>Quote Price</th>
8      </tr>
9      {% for quote in all_quotes %}
10         <tr class="quoterow {% cycle '' 'altrow' %}">
11             <td>{{ quote.id }}</td>
12             <td>{{ quote.name }}</td>
13             <td>{{ quote.company }}</td>
14             <td>{{ quote.submitted|date:"m-d-y" }}</td>
15             <td>{{ quote.quotedate|date:"m-d-y"
   |default:"pending" }}</td>
16             <td>{{ quote.quoteprice|default:"--" }}
   </td>
17         </tr>
18     {% endfor %}
19 </table>
20 {% endblock content %}
```

The HTML in this code should be straight forward—we build a table and render each quote record as a row in the table. The additional style element in **line 4** is to stop Chrome overriding our CSS and putting a border around the table cells. This style could also be added to your CSS file, but is small enough to sit neatly in your template without affecting readability.

The important work is done by the `for` loop between **lines 9 and 18**. Each field in the quote record is rendered as a table cell with additional formatting added by Django template filters:

▸ **Line 14.** Applies the `date` filter to the quote submitted date. The format string "`m-d-y`" governs how the date will be displayed, e.g. 15th June, 2017 will display as "06-15-17".

▸ **Line 15.** Applies the same format string as submitted date to the date the job is quoted (`quotedate`). We are also adding the `default` filter. This filter sets the default for the `quotedate` field to the word "pending" which will be substituted when the quote date is blank.

▸ **Line 16.** Uses the `default` filter again; this time, the filter substitutes two dashes (`--`) when the quote price is zero.

One more thing to note before we move on—in **line 10** we are using the `cycle` template tag for the first time. `cycle` is a built-in template tag that alternates between all the values listed inside the tag.

`cycle` is extremely useful for applying CSS classes to alternate table rows, which is exactly what we are doing in this template code. In our case, the list only has two elements—a blank string (`''`) and the string "altrow".

When this template renders, the odd rows will have the class attribute set to "quoterow" and the even rows will have the class attribute set to "quoterow altrow".

Now that we have finished the template, we need to add some CSS to show our quotes in a nicely formatted table:

```
# \mfdw_root\static\main.css

# ...
```

```
1  .quotehdr th {
2      background-color: #4c4c4c;
3      color: white;
4      text-align: center;
5      padding: 8px 5px;
6      border: none;
7  }
8  .quoterow td {
9      padding: 5px 10px;
10 }
11 .altrow {
12     background-color: #e0e0e0
13 }
```

If you save your files and run the development server, your quote list page should look like Figure 12-2. The quote list looks great, but as you can see from Figure 12-2, there is something wrong with the menu—the rest of the site pages are missing. This is because, if you remember from our previous work, the page list is passed in as a context variable.

Django's generic views make passing in context information very easy by defining a special method called `get_context_data`. We can implement this special method in our `QuoteList` class as follows:

```
# \quotes\views.py
```

```
1  class QuoteList(ListView):
2      model = Quote
3      context_object_name = 'all_quotes'
4
5      def get_context_data(self, **kwargs):
6          context = super(QuoteList, self).get_context_
   data(**kwargs)
7          context['page_list'] = Page.objects.all()
8          return context
```

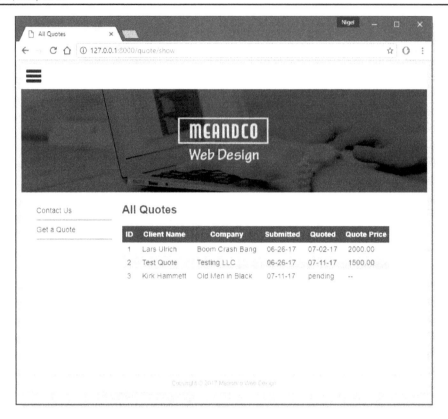

Figure 12-2. *The quote list is now nicely formatted, but most of the left side menu is missing because we haven't passed the page list to the template.*

By default, `get_context_data` merges all context data from any parent classes of the current class. To ensure that this behavior is preserved in our own classes, the context is first created by inheriting from the base class (**line 6**). In **line 7**, we are simply adding the `page_list` QuerySet to the context dictionary. That's all we need to do to add information to the context.

If you refresh your browser, all the menu items should appear. To add the quote list page, update your base template as follows (change in bold):

```
# \mfdw_site\templates\base.html

    {% endblock sidenav %}
    <li><a href="/contact">Contact Us</a></li>
    <li><a href="/quote/">Get a Quote</a></li>
    <li><a href="/quote/show">Show Quotes</a></li>
</ul>
```

Refresh your browser again and the completed quote list and menu should now show. See Figure 12-3 on page 200 for a view of the complete menu.

Viewing a Single Record with DetailView

The next step is to create a view to show an individual quote. We will implement the detail view with the list/detail idiom—when a user clicks a link in the list, our Django project will open the corresponding quote record.

There are a few steps to get the new detail view up and running, but they're all straight forward:

1. Create the new detail view—QuoteView;
2. Add a new URLconf that will display the detail view;
3. Create the detail view template;
4. Add some CSS so the detail view matches our site template; and
5. Modify the quote list template to link to the detail view.

Create the Detail View

Add the following view code to your views.py file (changes in bold):

```
# \quotes\views.py

from django.views.generic.list import ListView
from django.views.generic.detail import DetailView
```

```
# ...

1  class QuoteView(DetailView):
2      model = Quote
3      context_object_name = 'quote'
4
5      def get_context_data(self, **kwargs):
6          context = super(QuoteView, self).get_context_
   data(**kwargs)
7          context['page_list'] = Page.objects.all()
8          return context
```

As you can see, this code is almost identical to the list view code. At the top of the file, we add DetailView to the module imports. In **line 1** we are inheriting from the DetailView class to create our QuoteView. Like the QuoteList view, QuoteView is a simple class with a single get_context_data method (**lines 5 to 8**) that returns a list of pages for rendering the menu.

Add the URLconf

The next step is to modify the urls.py file in our quotes app (changes in bold):

```
# quotes\urls.py

1  from django.conf.urls import url
2
3  from . import views
4  from .views import QuoteList, QuoteView
5
6  urlpatterns = [
7      path('', views.quote_req, name='quote-request'),
8      path('show/<int:pk>', QuoteView.as_view(),
   name='quote-detail'),
9      path('/show', QuoteList.as_view(), name='show-
   quotes'),
10 ]
```

There are a couple of changes to the file. In **line 4** we are adding the QuoteView view to our imports. In **line 8** we are using another capturing group (See Chapter 9). The capturing group `<int:pk>` captures any integer at the end of the URL and passes it to the view in the parameter `pk` (primary key).

This is another of those little things Django does to make your life easier. If you pass a parameter named `pk` to a Django generic detail view, Django will automatically search the database for a record with a primary key equal to the value of `pk`. For example the URL `/quote/show/3` will search for a quote record with a primary key of "3".

Create the Detail View Template

Next, create a new file named `quote_detail.html` in your `templates` directory:

```
# \quotes\templates\quotes\quote_detail.html

1  {% extends "quotes/quote.html" %}
2
3  {% block title %}All Quotes{% endblock title %}
4
5  {% block content %}
6  <h1>Quote Detail</h1>
7
8  <table class="quote">
9    <tr><td>ID:</td><td>{{ quote.id }}</td></tr>
10   <tr><td>Name:</td><td>{{ quote.name }}</td></tr>
11   <tr><td>Company:</td><td>{{ quote.company }}</td></
   tr>
12   <tr><td>Email:</td><td>{{ quote.email }}</td></tr>
13   <tr><td>Web Address:</td><td>{{ quote.web }}</td></
   tr>
14   <tr><td>Job Description:</td><td>{{ quote.description
   }}</td></tr>
15   <tr><td>Site Status:</td><td>{{ quote.get_sitestatus_
   display }}</td></tr>
16   <tr><td>Priority:</td><td>{{ quote.get_priority_
```

```
      display }}</td></tr>
17    <tr><td>Submit Date:</td><td>{{ quote.
      submitted|date:"m-d-y" }}</td></tr>
18    <tr><td>Quote Date:</td><td>{{ quote.
      quotedate|date:"m-d-y"|default:"pending" }}</td></tr>
19    <tr><td>Quote Price:</td><td>{{ quote.
      quoteprice|default:"--" }}</td></tr>
20  </table>
21  <p><a href="../show">Back to quote list</a></p>
22  {% endblock content %}
```

This is all standard HTML and Django template tags; there is nothing that should be new to you except in **lines 15 and 16**.

When you set a `choices` field for a Django form widget, Django saves the value of the field to the database, not the human-readable name. For example, when the STATUS_CHOICES on the `sitestatus` field is set to "New Site", Django saves its value ("NEW") to the database.

When the value of `sitestatus` is retrieved from the database, this value would be passed to the template. Obviously, this is not what we want—we want to show the human-readable name.

Django makes this task easy by creating a special `get_FIELD_display()` method for each model field assigned a `choices` field. So, in our new view, `get_sitestatus_display` (**line 15**) is retrieving the human-readable name from the STATUS_CHOICES list and `get_priority_display` is retrieving the same from the PRIORITY_CHOICES list (**line 16**).

Add CSS to Format Detail View

Next, we want the detail view to match our site template and the list view, so we need to add a couple more CSS classes to our `main.css` file:

```
# \mfdw_site\static\main.css

# ...
```

```
.quote td:first-child {
    background-color: #4c4c4c;
    color: white;
    text-align: right;
    padding: 8px 5px;
    border: none;
}
.quote td {
    padding: 5px 10px;
}
```

There's nothing new here, it's plain CSS. Add the classes anywhere you like in your CSS file, although it's most logical to group them with the quote list classes.

Modify Quote List Template

Finally, we need to make a small change to the quote list template (change in bold):

```
# \quotes\templates\quotes\quote_list.html

# ...

{% for quote in all_quotes %}
        <tr class="quoterow {% cycle '' 'altrow' %}">
            <td><a href="show/{{ quote.id }}">{{ quote.id
}}</a></td>
            <td>{{ quote.name }}</td>

# ...
```

By adding the HTML anchor tag, we turn the quote ID at the beginning of each record in the quote list into a hyperlink that redirects to the detail view.

Fire up the development server and navigate to http://127.0.0.1:8000/quote/show. If all has gone according to plan, the quote ID's in the quote list will now be hyperlinks. Click on any one of these links and it should open a detail view of the selected quote (Figure 12-3).

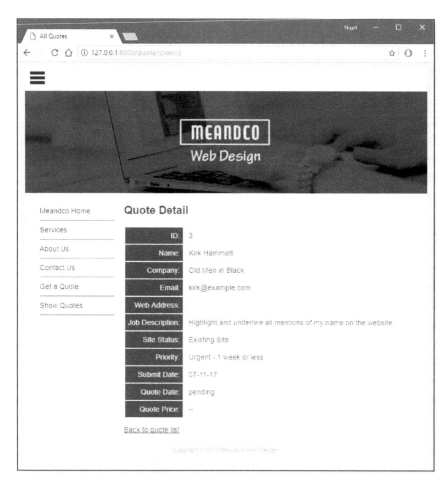

Figure 12-3. The completed quote detail template.

Chapter Summary

In this chapter, we learned about Django's generic class-based views. We learned how to implement two of Django's most important generic views—the list view and the detail view. We also learned how these generic views simplify the common programming task of showing a list of records and linking that list to the individual detail records.

There is one obvious problem with what we achieved this chapter. Did you spot it?

That's right, you would never show sensitive information like your quote records to anyone browsing your site. You need to have some sort of permission system in place to ensure private and sensitive information can only be seen by those who are authorized to see it. For example, site users should only be able to view information on the quotes they submitted.

This is the subject of the next chapter, where we will be implementing Django's built-in authentication and authorization system to limit what casual browsers can see on the site.

13

User Management

Most modern websites allow some kind of user interaction. Common examples include comments on blog posts, allowing users to customize the information they see, editorial control over content and e-commerce.

To make user management easier, Django comes with a user authentication and authorization system out of the box. With Django, you can both create and edit users in the admin, as well as add code to your views and templates to hide content from unauthorized users. In the first part of this chapter, we will look at how you can manage users in the admin, create user groups and assign permissions to a user or group.

In the last part of the chapter, we will modify our views so only registered users can submit a quote, as well as add a filter to the quote list so it only displays the quotes submitted by the logged in user. To accomplish this, we will be using Django's generic views and forms again to register users and log them in to our website.

Users in the Admin

Django's built-in authentication system is automatically added to the admin interface when you create a new project (Figure 13-1). With the admin you can:

- ▶ Add and delete users

- ▶ Edit existing users

- ▶ Reset user passwords

- ▶ Assign staff and/or superuser status to a user

- ▶ Add or remove user permissions

- ▶ Create user groups; and

- ▶ Add users to a group

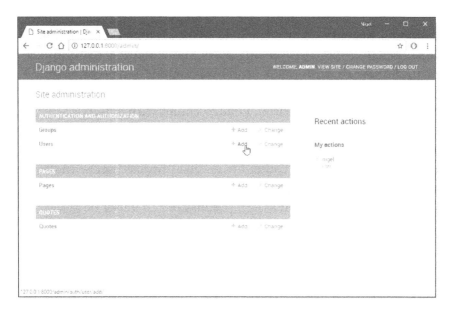

Figure 13-1. User and group management is added automatically to the admin. Users can be added directly from the admin home page.

Remember when we created an admin superuser (Chapter 7)? This special user has full access to all models in the admin and can add, change and delete any model record. In a real application, you will want to limit the number of users who have full access to your site.

Adding a new user is easy—click the green plus sign on the right of the **Users** entry on the admin home page. Enter a username and password and click save to add the new user.

Return to the admin home page and click **Users** to open the user list. Click on the username (Figure 13-2) to open the user edit screen.

Figure 13-2. *Select the new user from the list to edit the user's details.*

At the top of the user edit screen, you will see options to edit the user's password and personal info. Scroll down to the **Permissions** section and make sure **Staff status** is checked and **Superuser status** is unchecked (Figure 13-3).

What we have created here is considered a normal admin user. Normal admin users—that is, active, non-superuser staff members—are granted admin access through assigned permissions. Each object editable through the admin interface (e.g., quotes and pages) has four permissions: a create permission, a view permission, an edit permission and a delete permission.

Figure 13-3. Create a normal admin user (non-superuser) by making sure they are active and have staff status, but don't have superuser status.

Model Permissions

Note that these permissions are defined per-model, not per-object. For example, a user can be assigned permissions to change any quote, but not to change quotes submitted by a certain client.

Per-object permissions are a bit more complicated and outside the scope of this book, but are covered in the Django documentation[1].

Assigning permissions to a user grants the user access to do what is described by those permissions. When you create a user, that user has no permissions. It's up to you to give the user specific permissions.

We're going to do that now—we are going to create an author user who has permission to add and edit site pages, but not to delete them. Scroll down the edit page a bit further to the **User permissions** panel and add the following permissions using the horizontal filter (Figure 13-4):

```
pages|page|Can add page
pages|page|Can change page
```

---

1   https://docs.djangoproject.com/en/2.1/topics/auth/customizing/

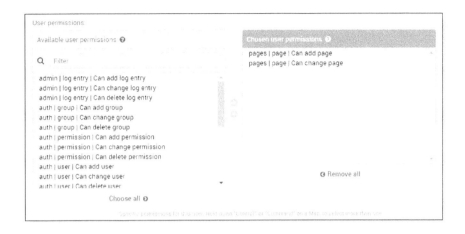

Figure 13-4. *Add permissions to the user by selecting in the horizontal filter and adding to the list. Multiple selections can be made by holding down the CTRL key (Command on a Mac).*

Once you have added the permissions, log out and log back in as the new user. The admin dashboard will now only show the pages app, hiding all the other models that the user doesn't have permission to access (Figure 13-5).

This is pretty easy, but what if you have many authors you want to add as users? It's time consuming to add permissions one at a time to each user. Luckily, Django allows you to create *user groups*, which is simply a group of permissions that can be added to a user all together, rather than one at a time.

Let's go ahead and create an author group. You will first have to log out as the author user and log back in as the admin user.

Figure 13-5. *The new user's permission setting limits their admin access to the pages app. If you open any page, you will also notice the delete button is hidden as they don't have delete permission.*

Creating a group is like creating a user—go to the admin front page and click the green add button to the right of the **Groups** listing and name your new group **Author**, add the permissions from the horizontal filter and save your new group (Figure 13-6).

Once you have added the group, you can go back to the user and edit their permissions to add the new group (Figure 13-7).

Don't forget to delete the permissions you assigned previously to prevent any permission clashes later. Save the user and now, when you log out and log back in again as the author user, they will have the same restricted view of the admin as we saw in Figure 13-5.

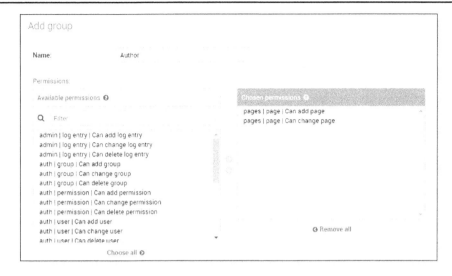

Figure 13-6. Create a user group and add permissions to the group using the horizontal filter. Multiple selections can be made by holding down the CTRL key (Command on a Mac).

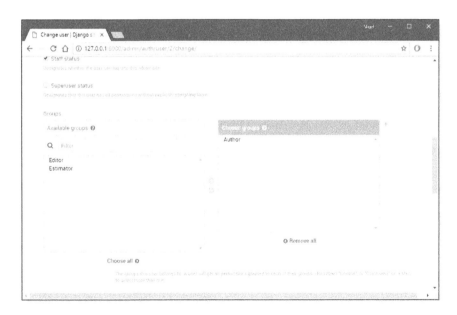

Figure 13-7. Adding a user to a group assigns all the group's permissions to the user.

That's about it for adding users and user permissions in the admin. You will notice in Figure 13-7, I have added two other groups—Editor and Estimator. I will leave them to you to create as a practice exercise. An editor should have the ability to add, edit and delete pages (whereas an author could only add and edit). An Estimator should have permission to edit a quote (to add quote information) but not add or delete quotes.

Users in the Front End

A common and important feature of modern websites is to hide content from unregistered users. To demonstrate how to restrict content to registered users in Django, we are going to implement an example of restricted access—site visitors must be registered to be able to submit and view quotes.

The first step in the process is to create the user registration system so that customers can register with the Meandco website. As managing users in the front end is such a common requirement, Django's developers have provided several handy classes and built-in forms and views to make registering and authenticating users a breeze.

To get our authentication system up and running, we need to do three things:

1. Create a customer registration view;
2. Create the authentication templates; and
3. Create new URLconfs to link to the authentication system.

Add the Registration View

Django has built-in generic authentication forms for logging users in and out and resetting or changing passwords. Each of these forms also has a built-in default view, so you don't have to create one. The UserCreationForm (which is used for registering new users with a website), however, doesn't have a default view—we need to write one.

We are going to create the user registration view with one of Django's generic editing views—CreateView. To create our new view, add the following to views.py (changes in bold):

```
# \quotes\views.py

# add the following to the imports at the top of the file
from django.views.generic.edit import CreateView
from django.contrib.auth.forms import UserCreationForm
from django.urls import reverse_lazy

# ...
```

```
1  class Register(CreateView):
2      template_name = 'registration/register.html'
3      form_class = UserCreationForm
4      success_url = reverse_lazy('register-success')
5
6      def form_valid(self, form):
7          form.save()
8          return HttpResponseRedirect(self.success_url)
```

CreateView is a useful class that makes creating and displaying a blank edit form easy—all you need to do is pass it a template and a form and it will create a blank edit form on the fly. First, we need to import CreateView and the UserCreationForm class into our quotes app's views.py file.

Then, we create the Register class. Stepping through this code:

▶ **Line 1.** The Register class declaration. The Register class inherits from CreateView.

▶ **Line 2.** The template_name attribute tells CreateView what template to use. We will create the register.html template shortly.

▶ **Line 3.** Is the form to use with CreateView. In this case, we're using the UserCreationForm class to create the form.

▶ **Line 4.** success_url is the URL that the form will redirect to once the form has been successfully processed. More on the reverse_lazy() function in the moment.

▸ **Lines 6 to 8.** Our `Register` class has a single method—
  `form_valid()`. This is a built-in method that will save our new user's
  information to the database once a valid registration form has been
  submitted. The `form_valid()` method then redirects to a success page
  URL set at runtime by reverse lookup.

I have introduced a new function in this bit of code—`reverse_lazy()`. In
keeping with the Don't Repeat Yourself (DRY) principle, it's always
advisable to avoid hard-coding URLs. Django makes this task easy by
providing the functions `reverse()` and `reverse_lazy()` for reversing
URLs. In other words, if you provide either `reverse()` or
`reverse_lazy()` with the name of the URL, it will look up the URL
name and replace it with the corresponding absolute URL.

We have been preparing to use reversible URLs ahead of time by naming
our URLs. For example, with the URLconf:

```
path('show', QuoteList.as_view(), name='show-quotes')
```

If we were to call `reverse('show-quotes')` at runtime, it would return
the URL `http://127.0.0.1:8000/quotes/show` (assuming the code
was still running on Django's development server).

This allows for highly flexible and dynamic URL generation, however it
has a drawback—when a class or a function is compiled, Django doesn't
know what the absolute URL is as it's not available until runtime.

Python solves this problem quite neatly with *lazy evaluation*. Put simply,
lazy evaluation will only compute the value (in this case the URL) when
needed.

In our `Register` class, Django's `reverse_lazy()` function implements
Python's lazy evaluation to wait until runtime to calculate the URL for
`success_url`. `register-success` is the name of the URLconf that we
will create a bit later in the chapter.

As a final exercise, compare the code in this class-based view with the code in the `quote_req` function. You can see that, in some cases, using generic views can reduce the amount of code needed quite substantially.

Create the Templates

Our next task is to create the templates for rendering our registration and login/logout forms. There are three templates that need to be created:

1. `login.html`. A template to display the login form;
2. `register.html`. A template to display the user registration form; and
3. `success.html`. A simple template to tell the user they have successfully registered with the site.

We will also make a modification to `base.html` to show user information at the top of the page.

Before creating the templates, create a new folder called `registration` in your site templates folder.

The Login Template

```
# mfdw_site\templates\registration\login.html

1   {% extends "base.html" %}
2
3   {% block title %}Quote Login{% endblock title %}
4
5   {% block sidenav %}
6       <li><a href="/">Home</a></li>
7   {% endblock sidenav %}
8
9   {% block content %}
10  <h1>Please Login</h1>
11  <p>You must be logged in to submit or view quotes.</p>
12
13  <form method="post" action="{% url 'login' %}">
```

```
14  <table>
15      {{ form.as_table }}
16      <tr>
17          <td> </td>
18          <td><input type="submit" value="login"></td>
19      </tr>
20  </table>
21  <p>Not registered yet? <a href="{% url 'register'
    %}">Register here</a>.</p>
22  <input type="hidden" name="next" value="{{ next }}" />
23  {% csrf_token %}
24  </form>
25
26  {% endblock content %}
```

This is mostly HTML and Django template code, but there are some lines that need some explanation:

▶ **Lines 13 and 21.** We are using Django's {% url %} tag. This tag performs exactly the same function as reverse_lazy()—it performs a reverse lookup of the URL name and replaces it with the actual URL when Django renders the template.

▶ **Line 22.** We've added a hidden field to the form. When a page link is redirected (which is what happens when a user is sent to the login page), Django will save the original destination in the next template variable. We're adding the next variable so that, once the form has been successfully submitted, the value of next is preserved and Django knows where to redirect the user.

The Register Template

```
# mfdw_site\templates\registration\register.html

{% extends "base.html" %}

{% block title %}User Registration{% endblock title %}

{% block sidenav %}
    <li><a href="/">Home</a></li>
{% endblock sidenav %}
```

```
{% block content %}
<h1>User Registration</h1>
<p>Enter your username and password to register.</p>

<form method="post" action="">
<table>
    {{ form.as_table }}
    <tr>
        <td> </td>
        <td><input type="submit" value="register"></td>
    </tr>
</table>
<input type="hidden" name="next" value="{{ next }}" />
{% csrf_token %}
</form>

{% endblock content %}
```

There's nothing new here, so you should find this template code easy to follow.

The Success Template

```
# mfdw_site\templates\registration\success.html

{% extends "base.html" %}

{% block title %}User Registration Success{% endblock
title %}

{% block sidenav %}
    <li><a href="/">Home</a></li>
{% endblock sidenav %}

{% block content %}
<h1>User Registration Success</h1>
<p>You have successfully registered.</p>

<p>Click <a href="{% url 'login' %}?next=/">here</a> to
log in.</p>

{% endblock content %}
```

Again, nothing new—just note how we are appending `?next=/` to the URL that is provided in a reverse lookup by the `{% url %}` tag. It's perfectly legal to concatenate text in this way in Django template code.

Modify the Base Template

Finally, we need to make some changes to `base.html` to display user authentication status at the top of the page (changes in bold):

```
# \mfdw_site\templates\base.html
```

```
1   <div id="logo"><img src="{% static 'logo.jpg' %}"
    alt=""/>
2       <span style="float: right;">
3           {% if user.is_authenticated %}
4               Hello, {{ user.username }}. <a href="{% url
    'logout' %}?next=/">Log out</a>.
5           {% else %}
6               Not logged in. <a href="{% url
    'login' %}?next=/">Log in</a>.
7           {% endif %}
8       </span>
9   </div>
10      <div id="topbanner"> # ...
```

This is simple to follow—on **line 3** we have an `if` statement that will render a logged in message if the user is logged in, or a logged out message if they are not (**lines 4 and 6** respectively). The template also provides a convenient link to login or logout directly from the page header.

Create URLconfs

Our third task is to add the URLconfs for our authentication views (changes in bold):

```
#  \mfdw_site\urls.py

# add the following to the imports at the top of the file
from django.views.generic import TemplateView
from quotes.views import Register

#  ...
```

```
1  urlpatterns = [
2      # ...
3      path('register/success/',TemplateView.as_
   view(template_name="registration/success.html"), name
   ='register-success'),
4      path('register/', Register.as_view(), name='register'),
5      path('quote/', include('quotes.urls')),
6      path('', include('django.contrib.auth.urls')),
7      path('', include('pages.urls')),
8  ]
```

Let's have a quick look at what's going on here:

▶ **Line 3.** We are using the `TemplateView` generic view from Chapter 12 to render a simple template when a user successfully registers with our site.

▶ **Line 4.** Is the URLconf for our user registration form.

▶ **Line 6.** We are including Django's authentication URLs which provide the URL and view for our login and logout views. A number of other URLs are loaded with `auth.urls` that we are not using in this book. If you want to dig further into the `auth.urls` and the cool generic authorization views they give you access too, check out the Django documentation[2].

---

2   https://docs.djangoproject.com/en/2.1/topics/auth/default/#module-django.contrib.auth. views

Testing the Authentication System

We have made quite a few changes to the front end, so now it's time to test to see it all works. Fire up the development server and navigate to `http://127.0.0.1:8000/`. At the top of the page, you should now see the logged out message (Figure 13-8).

Figure 13-8. The top of our modified base template showing the logged out message.

If you're running the development server from earlier in the chapter and are still logged in as admin, you will see a message like Figure 13-9. If you do see this message, click on **Log out** so we can test the quote views.

Figure 13-9. The top of our modified base template showing the logged in message.

Click on the "Log in" link in the menu and the site should now redirect to the login page (Figure 13-10).

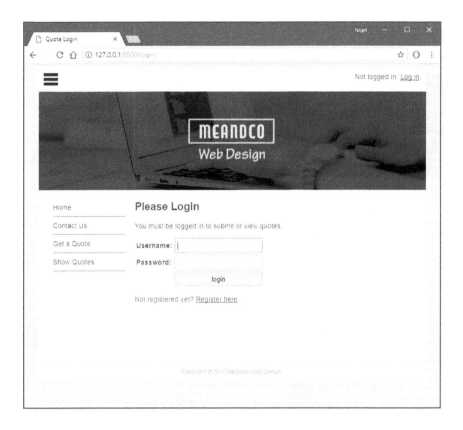

Figure 13-10. *The login template. Note the link to the registration template at the bottom of the form.*

Finally, on the login form click the **Register here** link and you should see the user registration page (Figure 13-11).

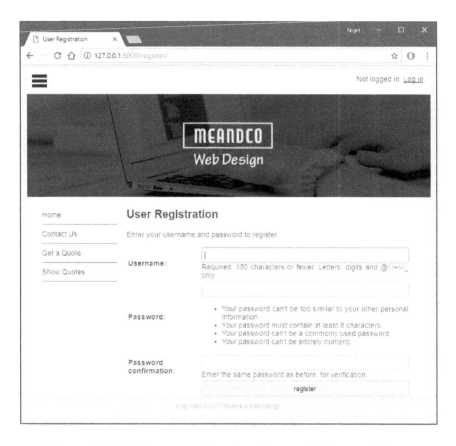

Figure 13-11. *The user registration form and all its validation logic is generated automatically for you by Django.*

Restricting Users in the Front End

Now that we have set up the authentication system, all we need to do to restrict user access in the front end is to modify the views to ensure that only logged in users can access the quote system.

To require site visitors to log in before they can submit or view quotes, we must modify the views for our quote form and for our quote list display. These views are:

1. The quote request (`quote_req`) view;
2. The quote list (`QuoteList`) view; and
3. The quote detail (`QuoteView`) view.

Django includes built-in functionality that makes this task simple. However, we use two different approaches because `quote_req` is a function-based view whereas `QuoteList` and `QuoteView` are class-based views.

Decorators and Mixins

Decorators and mixins are powerful features of Python and Django, which you will find yourself using regularly in your career as a Python/Django programmer.

They are also a huge topic; I will only touch on a small set of their capabilities in this chapter. I encourage you to expand your understanding of these powerful tools.

The Python wiki[3] has some great information on decorators in Python. Django uses decorators in several modules. More information can be found in the Django documentation[4].

Mixins are not specific to Python, so multiple references can be found online. Django uses mixins extensively in class-based views, which are covered in detail in the Django documentation[5].

---

3   https://wiki.python.org/moin/PythonDecorators
4   https://docs.djangoproject.com/en/2.1/search/?q=decorators
5   https://docs.djangoproject.com/en/2.1/topics/class-based-views/mixins/

Modify the Quote Request View

To modify `quote_req` we are going to add a *decorator*. A decorator is a special function that wraps around another function and modifies its behavior. In Python, a decorator function starts with the @ symbol and must be on the line immediately before the function it modifies.

This concept is easier to understand in practice, so let's go ahead and modify our `quote_req` function (changes in bold):

```
# \quotes\views.py

# add the following to the imports at the top of the file
from django.contrib.auth.decorators import login_required

# ...

@login_required(login_url=reverse_lazy('login'))
def quote_req(request):

    # ...
```

Here we have imported the `login_required` function and used it to wrap (decorate) the `quote_req` function. Now, when `quote_req` is called, `login_required` first checks if the user is logged in and redirects to the login view if they're not.

Because a decorator is a function, we need to use `reverse_lazy()` to ensure that Django doesn't try to evaluate the URL until runtime. So, when Django sees `reverse_lazy('login')`, it will convert it to the URL `login/` at runtime and append it to the root URL (in our case `http://127.0.0.1:8000/`).

In case you were wondering where the `login/` URL came from, when we included `django.contrib.auth.urls` earlier in this chapter, it included URL patterns for a number of built-in views, including:

```
^login/$ [name='login']
```

Clever stuff. URL reversing is one of those things about Django you really grow to love when you are trying to build portable and scalable applications.

Moving on, we also want the `quote_req` view to save the user information with the quote when it's submitted. To add the current user's username to the quote, make the following modifications to your `quote_req` view (changes in bold):

```
1   def quote_req(request):
2       submitted = False
3       if request.method == 'POST':
4           form = QuoteForm(request.POST, request.FILES)
5
6
7           if form.is_valid():
8               quote = form.save(commit=False)
9               try:
10                  quote.username = request.user
11              except Exception:
12                  pass
13              quote.save()
14              return HttpResponseRedirect('/quote/?
    submitted=True')
15
16          # ...
```

This might seem a little confusing at first, so I have numbered the important lines so we can step through them:

▶ **Line 8.** Set the `commit` property of the `save()` method to `False`. This creates a new instance of the `Quote` model without saving the record to the database.

▶ **Line 10.** Django will pass information on the current user to the view in the `request` object, so this line sets the `username` field in the quote model instance to `request.user`. To ensure the view doesn't crash if `request.user` is not set, the line is wrapped in a `try/except` clause that will leave `username` blank in case of error.

▶ **Line 13.** The record is saved to the database.

Modify the Quote List View

Next, we modify the `QuoteList` class to only show quotes submitted by the logged in user. This is another simple process, however, this time we will be using a *mixin*.

A mixin is a special kind of class that contains class methods that can be "mixed in" to other classes without them needing to inherit from the mixin class. We have already used a mixin when we first created the `QuoteList` view—the `get_context_data` method from Django's `MultipleObjectMixin`.

Let's make the modifications to our `QuoteList` view, and then I will explain what's going on (changes in bold):

```
# \quotes\views.py

# add the following to the imports at the top of the file
from django.contrib.auth.mixins import LoginRequiredMixin

# ...

1  class QuoteList(LoginRequiredMixin, ListView):
2      login_url = reverse_lazy('login')
3      # model = Quote comment or remove this line
4      context_object_name = 'all_quotes'
5
6      def get_queryset(self):
7          return Quote.objects.filter(
   username=self.request.user)
```

First, we are adding a new import at the top of the file to import the `LoginRequiredMixin`. I have numbered a few lines so we can step through them:

▶ **Line 1.** We are adding `LoginRequiredMixin` to the class declaration.
▶ **Line 2.** We provide the login URL to the class. This is functionally identical to passing the login URL to the decorator in a function-based view. Note we have used the `reverse_lazy()` function again to

evaluate the login URL at runtime, rather than hard-code it into the view.

▶ **Line 6**. Is another mixin. get_queryset will return a list of quotes filtered to include only those quotes that were submitted by the logged in user.

Modify the Quote Detail View

The changes we need to make to the quote detail view are identical to the changes we made in the quote list view. As we have already imported the LoginRequiredMixin class, all we need do is make the changes in the class:

```
# \quotes\views.py

1   class QuoteView(LoginRequiredMixin, DetailView):
2       login_url = reverse_lazy('login')
3       # model = Quote
4       context_object_name = 'quote'
5
6       def get_queryset(self):
7           return Quote.objects.filter(username=self.
    request.user)

    # ...
```

You might be wondering why we are adding a QuerySet that filters the quotes to only include quotes from the current user when we are retrieving a single record. This is because LoginRequiredMixin only checks if the user is logged in, it doesn't check if the user has permission to access the quote.

For example, if the logged in user enters a URL directly, say, 127.0.0.1:8000/quote/show/3. The quote with ID=3 will show regardless of whether the user submitted the quote or not.

Filtering by the current logged in user ensures that the quote belongs to that user. If not, the QuerySet will be empty and Django will throw a 404 (page not found) error.

You could also implement this so that Django sends some kind of "permission denied" message, but I prefer this implementation. It's neater, and the 404 error doesn't give a would-be hacker any information on whether something interesting might exist at that URL.

Once you have all the forms showing correctly, it's time to test the quote system by registering new users, submitting some quotes and viewing the list of quotes for each user.

As always, pay very close attention to what Django's error page says when something doesn't work. In 99% of cases the information you need to fix the error is on the error page.

Chapter Summary

At the beginning of this chapter, we learned how to add and edit users in the admin. We also learned how to assign user permissions and how to create user groups to simplify assigning multiple permissions to users.

In the second part of the chapter, we learned how to manage authentication in the front end by implementing an authentication and authorization system that limits access to the quote functionality of our site to registered users.

This chapter concludes the development phase of our website. We are now ready to release our masterpiece to the world and deploy the site to the Internet.

In the next chapter, we will be taking the steps necessary to package up our website and deploy it to Python Anywhere—a Python and Django hosting platform that allows you to deploy and test your site for free!

14

Deploying a Django Website

Now that we have completed the development of our website, it's time for the exciting part—deploying the code to a web server. Deploying a website can often be a complex and frustrating process, however, this is another area where Django makes things easier.

Django will run on any server that supports Python's Web Server Gateway Interface (WSGI)[1]. To run Django on a WSGI server only requires a single configuration file—wsgi.py.

Django also supports the three most popular Internet databases (MySQL, PostgreSQL and Oracle) out of the box with many third-party interfaces to both SQL and non-SQL database engines.

Choosing a Host

In this chapter, we will be using PythonAnywhere[2], mainly because they have a free beginner account that is perfect for demonstrating a live deployment without costing you any money.

I also chose PythonAnywhere because they have a deployment process that still requires you to do some setup. Many Django-friendly hosts now have "1-click" installs that, while convenient, don't teach you the mechanics of deploying a website.

---

1   http://wsgi.readthedocs.io/en/latest/
2   https://www.pythonanywhere.com/

If you are interested in exploring other options for Django hosting, I can personally recommend WebFaction[3]. I have been using them for 6 years without a fault. The `djangobook.com` website is hosted with them. Others I can recommend from experience are Heroku[4] and DigitalOcean[5].

Bottom line, any host that either supports Python directly, or where you can set up your own virtual server (which is most cloud-based servers these days), will support Django.

Preparing the Site for Deployment

Before we transfer the site files to the web server, we need to do some tidying up of the files in our project folders.

At this point, you can make a backup of your site files and work directly in your project folders, however, as I like to leave the local copy intact and running in case I need to troubleshoot, we will work with a zip file that will be uploaded to PythonAnywhere.

Navigate to the `\mfdw_project` folder and zip up the `\mfdw_root` folder. Your project tree should look like this when you are done:

```
\mfdw_project
    \env_mfdw
    \mfdw_root
    mfdw_root.zip
```

Now, open the zip file (don't extract!) and do the following:

1. Delete the `db.sqlite3` file from inside the `\mfdw_root` folder
2. Delete the `\uploads` folder from inside the `\mfdw_root` folder
3. Delete all files inside the `\quotes\migrations` folder

3   https://www.webfaction.com/
4   https://www.heroku.com/
5   https://www.digitalocean.com/

4. Delete all files inside the `\pages\migrations` folder

5. Save and close the zip file

The purpose of this tidy up is to remove the test database and delete all old migrations so we can generate a clean set of migrations to apply to our new MySQL database on the web server.

What if I Want to Migrate my Data?

Inevitably, you will need to migrate data from one database to another sometime in your programming career. However, we are not migrating data in this book simply because it's very error prone and almost never goes smoothly.

Good programming practice is to connect to a database like MySQL or PostgreSQL as early in the development cycle as possible to ease the transition to a production database.

This approach was not practical for this book. I wanted you to learn about Django without spending hours trouble-shooting database installations and data migrations, so we will deploy with a clean database.

Deploy to PythonAnywhere

The first step in deploying the website is to set up your account with PythonAnywhere. Go to `https://www.pythonanywhere.com` and create your free beginner account. Once you have created your account and logged in, you will be directed to your dashboard (Figure 14-1).

At the top of your dashboard are five tabs—**Consoles, Files, Web, Tasks** and **Databases**. We will be visiting four of these tabs in turn to set up your website.

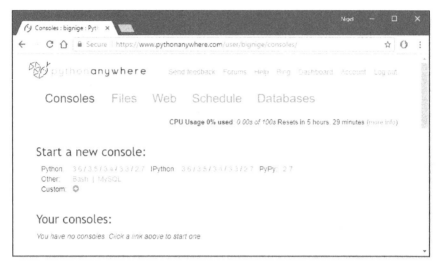

Figure 14-1. *Your PythonAnywhere dashboard provides tabbed pages where you can manage your files, web apps and databases.*

Add a Database

PythonAnywhere only provides the option to set up a MySQL database on a beginner account, so click on the Databases tab and scroll down to the **Create a database** section, enter mfdw_db as the database name and click Create (Figure 14-2).

Figure 14-2. *Adding a new MySQL database to your PythonAnywhere hosting account.*

You also need to create a password for your database, so scroll down a bit further and create a password for your new database (Figure 14-3).

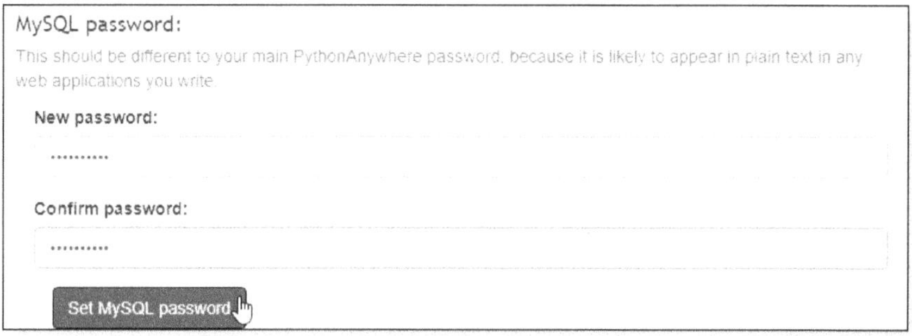

MySQL password:

This should be different to your main PythonAnywhere password, because it is likely to appear in plain text in any web applications you write.

New password:

··········

Confirm password:

··········

Set MySQL password

Figure 14-3. *To use the new database, you need to set a database password.*

Once you have set a new database password, write down the database host address (under **Connecting:** at the top of the **Databases** page), your username and the database name (if you didn't use mfdw_db). You will need them in the next section.

Upload the Site Files

Click on the **Files** tab in your dashboard and click on the **Upload a file** button and upload your zip file to the server. Once the zip file is uploaded, it will appear in your Files list (Figure 14-4).

To extract the site files, we need to open a console and run the unzip tool. PythonAnywhere has a few ways to open a console, but the easiest for this exercise is to click the "Open Bash console here" link at the top of the **Files** page (Figure 14-5).

Figure 14-4. *The server files list showing the uploaded zip file of your site files.*

Figure 14-5. *Opening a Bash console (command prompt) on PythonAnywhere Files tab.*

PythonAnywhere will open a new console window that looks like the Windows terminal or PowerShell window you are used to. At the command prompt, type:

```
$ unzip mfdw_root.zip
```

Don't type in the dollar sign ($)—this is there to show that you are entering a command at the Bash console prompt. If all has gone to plan, you will get a string of listings scrolling up the page as PythonAnywhere unzips your files to the server.

Install Django

Keeping with good programming practice, we will be running our website from inside a virtual environment, so first we must install one. Using the same console you opened in the last section, enter the following:

```
$ mkvirtualenv --python=/usr/bin/python3.6 env_mfdw
```

Note that we are using Python 3.6, not Python 3.7. This is because, at the time or writing, PythonAnywhere doesn't offer Python 3.7. This will not be a problem—Django 2.1 runs fine on Python 3.6. Once the virtual environment has installed, it will start automatically, giving you the familiar bracketed command prompt:

```
(env_mfdw) [timestamp] ~ $
```

The [timestamp] will show the current server time. Now it's time to install Django into the virtual environment:

```
(env_mfdw) [] ~ $ pip install "django>=2.1,<2.2"
```

The output from the Bash console will be similar to when we installed Django locally in Chapter 4. pip will automatically install the latest version of Django 2.1 (2.1 at the time of writing).

As we are using a virtual environment, we also need to install the Python database client for MySQL, so do that now while we are still in the console:

```
(env_mfdw) [timestamp] ~ $ pip install mysqlclient
```

Install the Web App

Return to the dashboard, click on the **Web** tab and then click **Add a new web app**. A series of windows will open prompting you for more information:

1. Click **Next**

2. Select **Manual configuration**. (DON'T select Django!)

3. Select **Python 3.6**

4. Click **Next**

PythonAnywhere will then create the new app for you. When the page refreshes, scroll down to the **Virtualenv:** section and click on "Enter path to a virtualenv, if desired" link. You will be prompted to enter a path to your virtual environment. Enter env_mfdw into the box and click the check button. PythonAnywhere will replace it with the full path to your virtual environment (Figure 14-6).

Figure 14-6. Link your web application to the Python virtual environment where your Django site will run. Note the "Start a console" link. You will be using this soon.

Configure the Web App

Now the web app is installed, we need to configure the WSGI file and Django's settings to run on the web host.

While still on the **Web** tab, scroll down to the **Code:** section and open the wsgi.py file (Figure 14-7). Note that this isn't the wsgi.py file from your project—the PythonAnywhere server ignores that file.

Figure 14-7. PythonAnywhere has its own wsgi.py file that must be configured correctly for your Django site to run.

PythonAnywhere will open the file in an editor in your browser. Delete everything in the file except the ++ DJANGO ++ section and then uncomment the relevant sections. I have reproduced the modified file below. Most of the comments have been removed to make it clear which lines need to be uncommented:

```
import os
import sys

path = '/home/<yourusername>/mfdw_root'
if path not in sys.path:
    sys.path.append(path)

os.environ['DJANGO_SETTINGS_MODULE'] = 'mfdw_site.settings'

# then, for django >=1.5:
from django.core.wsgi import get_wsgi_application
application = get_wsgi_application()
```

The two lines that need to be changed are listed in bold:

1. Add your project path to Django's path statement; and

2. Tell the WSGI server application where to find your Django app's settings file.

Make sure you save the file after you make the changes. Return to the dashboard and select the **Files** tab. Navigate to your mfdw_site directory and open your settings.py file. Make the changes in bold and then save the file:

```
# yourusername/mfdw_root/mfdw_site/settings.py

# ...

ALLOWED_HOSTS = ['<yourusername>.pythonanywhere.com']

# ...

# Database
# https://docs.djangoproject.com/en/2.1/ref/
settings/#databases

DATABASES = {
    'default': {
        'ENGINE': 'django.db.backends.mysql',
        'NAME': '<yourusername>$mfdw_db',
        'USER': '<yourusername>',
        'PASSWORD': '<yourpassword>',
        'HOST':
'<yourusername>.mysql.pythonanywhere-services.com',
    }
}

# ...

STATIC_ROOT = '/home/<yourusername>/mfdw_site/static'
```

The changes to the database connection settings are straight forward, just enter the settings I suggested you write down earlier. If you forgot to write down the settings, open your **Databases** tab in a new window and copy and paste the settings into the file.

The STATIC_ROOT path provides the necessary path statement for the collectstatic management tool we will be using shortly.

Run Django Management Commands

Next, we have a few Django management commands to run. Return to the **Web** tab, scroll down to **Virtualenv:** and click on the "Start a console in this virtualenv" link. When the virtual environment is running in the console, change into the project folder:

```
(env_mfdw) [timestamp] ~ $ cd mfdw_root
```

Once in the site folder, we need to make and run the migrations to set our models up in the database. First we tell Django to create new initial migrations for our pages and quotes apps:

```
$ python manage.py makemigrations pages quotes
```

Then we run all migrations:

```
$ python manage.py migrate
```

For static files (CSS, JavaScript and templates) to work correctly in production, Django requires that they all be collected into one folder. The collectstatic management command does this automatically for you:

```
$ python manage.py collectstatic
```

Finally, our new database needs an admin user, so create one using the createsuperuser command we used in Chapter 4:

```
$ python manage.py createsuperuser
```

Link to the Static Files

Exit the console and return to the **Web** tab on the PythonAnywhere dashboard. Scroll down to the **Static files:** section and add the following:

▶ **Enter URL:** Add your STATIC_URL (/static/)
▶ **Enter Path:** Add the same path as you entered in settings.py

When you have entered your static files setting correctly, your **Static files:** should look like Figure 14-8.

Figure 14-8. Your PythonAnywhere Static files settings pointing to the folder where the collectstatic command saved all your static files.

Once you have saved the static files setting, scroll back to the top of the page and click on the big green **Reload** button.

Add a Home Page

If you tried to navigate to
http://<yourusername>.pythonanywhere.com now you would get an error. This is because we have not added any pages to our new website. Go to http://<yourusername>.pythonanywhere.com/admin/, log in with the superuser account you created and add the following page:

▶ **Title:** Home
▶ **Permalink:** /
▶ Add and update date and some content

Save the page and click on **VIEW SITE** from within the Django admin. If all has gone to plan, you should see your home page.

Set Site to Production Mode

The final, but most important task to complete is to secure your site for production use. This requires two changes to your settings.py file:

1. Generate a new secret key; and
2. Set debug mode to False.

Before we go and edit our settings file, let's generate a new secret key. The simplest way to do this is to run the virtual environment we used for developing the website on your local machine and create a dummy project:

```
(env_mfdw) ...mfdw_project> django-admin startproject dummy
```

Once the dummy project has been created, you can simply copy the secret key from the settings file, and add to your production file, then delete the dummy project.

Another way to generate a new secret key is to generate it manually using the same code that Django uses internally to generate secret keys. From within a standard Python shell, enter the following:

```
>>> import random
>>> hash = 'abcdefghijklmnopqrstuvwxyz0123456789!@#$%^&*(-_=+)'
>>> ''.join(random.SystemRandom().choice(hash) for i in range(50))
'r&$s#!8bimjo+$9f37!2bs%budc3s56v_1d_^cpde2ohf#u#o1'
```

The last line is the generated secret key. It will be different every time you run the code. Copy this secret key to your production settings.

DON'T Use Online Key Generators!

There are many sites where you can generate secret keys online. I don't recommend this for obvious reasons—how do you know the site is not saving a list of keys that have been generated to use in brute force attacks on websites?

Answer is you don't, so it's not worth the risk.

Once you have generated a new secret key, return to the PythonAnywhere dashboard and select the **Files** tab. Navigate to your my_site directory, open your settings.py file and make the changes below:

```
# SECURITY WARNING: keep the secret key used in
production secret!
SECRET_KEY = 'paste your new key here'
# SECURITY WARNING: don't run with debug turned on in
production!
DEBUG = False
```

You now have a production-ready website deployed and ready to show to the world. Well done!

A final note of caution though.

The PythonAnywhere beginner account should not be considered for a production website—it's severely limited in both bandwidth and being able to access third-party websites. If you want to use your website project for a live web application, you should either upgrade your PythonAnywhere to a paid account or try one of the many other web hosts that support Django.

Chapter Summary

In this chapter, we have taken our completed website and deployed it to a web host. During deployment we carried out common website deployment tasks like setting up a production database, migrating our models, copying project files to the server, configuring the server to serve our application and securing our site for production.

Of course, there is much more to deploying a more complicated web application into a real production environment. For example, we have not configured a mail server so that our contact form can send emails, rather than dump the response to the console.

In the next chapter, I will be providing you with a few tips and resources for continuing your Django programming journey.

How did you go?

I sincerely hope that you have managed to get this far and not only know a whole lot more about Django, but are also the proud owner of an awesome new website.

If you enjoyed the book, I would greatly appreciate it if you could leave a review on Amazon for me.

Your feedback is not only appreciated, but will help others decide if this is the right book for them.

You can leave a review by going to:

https://www.amazon.com/review/create-review?&asin= B07GWJSSLN

All the best with your programming journey!

Nige

15

Next Steps

You have come a long way in your journey to becoming a Django programmer. You now have the skills to create your own basic website from scratch and deploy it to the Internet.

There is, however, a lot more to learn to get the most out of Django. As I said at the beginning of this book, Django is a very large and powerful framework that has been used to create some of the most popular websites on the Internet today.

To help you further along your journey, I have put together this short chapter to outline what I believe should be your next steps along the path to becoming a Django expert.

Testing

You have been testing code right throughout this book, maybe without realizing it. Each time you use the Django shell to see if a function works, or to see what output you get for a given input, you are testing your code.

Testing is a normal part of application development, however, what's different in automated tests is that the testing work is done for you by the system. You create a set of tests once, and then as you make changes to your app, you can check that your code still works as you originally intended; without having to perform time consuming manual testing.

Like all mature programming languages, Django provides inbuilt unit testing capabilities. Unit testing is a software testing process where individual units of a software application are tested to ensure they do what they are expected to do.

Unit testing can be performed at multiple levels—from testing an individual method to see if it returns the right value and how it handles invalid data, up to testing a whole suite of methods to ensure a sequence of user inputs leads to the desired results.

Software testing is a deep and detailed subject, so I have not covered it in any detail in this book. If you only ever create simple web applications like the website we have created in this book, you could probably get away with not creating automatic tests for your applications. However, if you wish to become a professional programmer and work on more complex projects, you need to know how to create automated tests.

There are many resources on the Internet on software testing theory and methods; I encourage you to do your own research on this important topic. For a more detailed discussion on Django's approach to unit testing, see the Django Project website[1]. I also have a whole chapter on testing in Django in my Django reference book—*Mastering Django: Core*. See djangobook.com for more detail on where you can get the book.

Documenting Your Code

While it's every programmer's least favorite job, documenting your code is an essential part of being a professional programmer—especially when your apps start to get more complicated.

I have used comments on many occasions throughout this book to illustrate or explain a section of code. I encourage you to use comments in the same manner in your code.

---

1   https://docs.djangoproject.com/en/2.1/topics/testing/

Perhaps more important than adding explanatory comments throughout your code, is using docstrings to annotate your classes, functions and methods. I introduced docstrings in Chapter 5, but to jog your memory:

```
"""This is a single line docstring"""

"""
This is a multi-line
docstring
"""
```

Docstrings are used to describe the various Python objects in our applications and are compiled into the special __doc__() attribute by the Python compiler.

Getting into the habit of using docstrings to describe your modules, classes, functions and methods also allows you to maximize the usefulness of Django's built-in admin documentation generator[2]. The documentation generator creates complete documentation for all your models and apps automatically, which can be a huge time-saver.

Connecting to Other Databases

While Django officially supports PostgreSQL, MySQL, Oracle and SQLite, there are several libraries and packages that allow you to connect Django to your database of choice. An Internet search for Django and your database name is usually a good start. StackOverflow is another good resource to see what tools and tips are available for connecting to other databases.

Django will also connect to some of the so-called NoSQL databases. A good place to start is the Django Packages website[3].

2   https://docs.djangoproject.com/en/2.1/ref/contrib/admin/admindocs/
3   https://djangopackages.org/grids/g/nosql/

While on the subject of databases, there is an important thing you must consider before embarking on your next project. While we developed the entire website in this book using SQLite and then created a new MySQL database for deployment, this is often not practical for a production site.

As soon as you have the need to enter production information that must be exported to the live database, you are better off continuing development using the same database you will be using in production.

As I noted in the last chapter, data migration is a fraught process and almost never goes to plan. To minimize frustration and delays to your project, it's always best to develop in the same database as you will be using in production.

To use a production database in development doesn't necessarily mean you have to install the database server to your local machine. Most inexpensive hosting plans allow you to create databases. Using MySQL or PostgreSQL in development can be as simple as setting up a development database on your host and then exporting or cloning your development database to production when complete.

Django's "App Store"

I introduced the Django Packages[4] website in Chapter 2. Noted here as a reminder that much of what you are ever likely to need to do in Django has been done before. The Django Packages site is not just a useful resource for obtaining free Django apps to install into your website. As all the apps contain full source code, you can use them as the basis for your own custom app, or you can improve an existing app and contribute to improving open source apps like many developers before you.

---

4   https://djangopackages.org/

Online Django Resources

There are dozens of quality Django resources online. The first and primary resource should always be the official Django documentation[5].

It's considered a rite of passage for all serious Django developers to have completed the full Django tutorial before being allowed to ask a question on any Django forum. While the tutorial does have its quirks, it's fundamental to understanding the basics of Django. It's also the resource that is most referenced in other Django tutorials (e.g., the infamous `polls` app).

If you are interested in further exploring content that I have written, the place to go is `djangobook.com`. I post a huge number of free tutorials, tips and tricks for programming Django. The site is also home of the free online version of *Mastering Django: Core*, my complete Django reference manual.

There are a variety of other free resources published online, however quality can be variable and, as Django is always in active development, can get out of date quickly. I have found the best place to go is the Django *Python Web Framework* group on Facebook. The group admins have published a resource list that is continually updated.

Other resources for Django related help:

▶   The Django users Google group[6]
▶   Django's IRC channel[7]
▶   Django on Stack Overflow[8]

---

5   https://docs.djangoproject.com/en/2.1/
6   https://groups.google.com/forum/#!forum/django-users
7   irc://irc.freenode.net/django
8   https://stackoverflow.com/questions/tagged/django

Django Books

At the time of writing, there are very few books available for Django 2. The only book covering Django 2 that I can confidently recommend (besides this one of course!) is *Django for Beginners*[9] by Will Vincent.

Two Scoops of Django 1.11[10] is also highly recommended. Django 1.11 LTS is fully supported by the Django development team for at least another two years. Keep in mind that this is not a beginner's book, however, if you learn all the material in this book, Danny and Audrey's book will be a valuable addition to your learning.

The Second Edition of my own Django reference, *Mastering Django: Core* will be released in 2019. The Second Edition will be a full update of the original code from Django 1.8 LTS to Django 2.2 LTS.

More information on the release date and contents will be published on djangobook.com in the coming months.

A Final Request

Learning to program is often a frustrating and difficult exercise, but that moment when the light goes on in your mind and you finally work it out is one of the best feelings you can have in any career.

Once you have completed all the material in this book and have a website you can be proud of, I would love it if you shared your experience with me by sending me an email to nigel@masteringdjango.com.

Thank you so much!

Big Nige

August 2018

---

9   https://djangoforbeginners.com/

10   https://www.twoscoopspress.com/products/two-scoops-of-django-1-11

Additional Reference Material

This appendix contains additional reference material on models and forms.

Table A-2. *Common Field Types*

Type	Description
BooleanField	A true/false field.
CharField	A string field, for small- to large-sized strings. max_length option is required.
DateField	A date, represented in Python by a datetime.date instance. Has two extra, optional arguments: auto_now which automatically set the field to now every time the object is saved, and auto_now_add which automatically set the field to now when the object is first created.
DateTimeField	A date and time, represented in Python by a datetime.datetime instance. Takes the same extra arguments as DateField.
DecimalField	A fixed-precision decimal number, represented in Python by a Decimal instance. Has two required arguments: max_digits and decimal_places.

Table A-2. Common Field Types

Type	Description
EmailField	A CharField that checks that the value is a valid email address.
FileField	A file upload field.
FloatField	A floating-point number.
ImageField	Inherits all attributes and methods from FileField, but also validates that the uploaded object is a valid image. Additional height and width attributes. Requires the Pillow library.
IntegerField	An integer.
TextField	A large text field. If you specify a max_length attribute, it will be reflected in the Textarea widget of the auto-generated form field. However it is not enforced at the model or database level.
TimeField	A time, represented in Python by a datetime. time instance. Accepts the same auto-population options as DateField.
URLField	A CharField for a URL. Optional max_length argument. If you don't specify max_length, a default of 200 is used.

Table A-3. Common Field Options.

Option	Description
null	If True, Django will store empty values as NULL in the database. Default is False.
blank	If True, the field is allowed to be blank. Default is False.

Table A-3. Common Field Options.

Option	Description
choices	An iterable (e.g., a list or tuple) consisting itself of iterables of exactly two items (e.g. `[(A, B), (A, B) ...]`) to use as choices for this field.
default	The default value for the field. This can be a value or a callable object.
editable	If `False`, the field will not be displayed in the admin or any other model form. They are also skipped during model validation. Default is `True`.
help_text	Extra help text to be displayed with the form widget.
primary_key	If `True`, this field is the primary key for the model. If you don't specify `primary_key=True` for any field in your model, Django will automatically add the primary key.
unique	If `True`, this field must be unique throughout the table. This is enforced at the database level and by model validation.
verbose_name	A human-readable name for the field. If the verbose name isn't given, Django will automatically create it using the field's attribute name, converting underscores to spaces.

Table A-4. More Common Built-n Template Tags

Tag	Description
comment	Ignores everything between {% comment %} and {% endcomment %}.
cycle	Produces one of its arguments each time this tag is encountered. Useful for tasks like applying alternating styles to table rows, or list items. E.g. `<tr class="{% cycle rowvalue1 rowvalue2 %}">`
debug	Outputs a whole load of debugging information, including the current context and imported modules.
firstof	Outputs the first argument variable that is not False. Outputs nothing if all the passed variables are False. Sample usage:{% firstof var1 var2 var3 %}
for ... empty	The for tag can take an optional {% empty %} clause whose text is displayed if the given array is empty or could not be found.
If/elif/else	The {% if %} tag evaluates a variable, and if that variable is true the contents of the block are output. The if tag may take one or several {% elif %} clauses, as well as an {% else %} clause that will be displayed if all previous conditions fail. These clauses are optional.
include	Loads a template and renders it with the current context. This is a way of including other templates within a template.
now	Displays the current date and/or time, using a format according to the given string.
url	Returns an absolute path reference matching a given view function and optional parameters. E.g. {% url 'some-url-name' v1 v2 %}. The first argument is a path to a view function. Additional arguments are optional and should be space-separated values that will be used as arguments in the URL.

Table A-5. More Common Built-in Template Filters

Filter	Description
add	Adds the argument to the value. For example: `{{ value|add:"2" }}`
addslashes	Adds slashes before quotes. Useful for escaping strings in CSV, for example. For example: `{{ value|addslashes }}`
center	Centers the value in a field of a given width. For example: `{{ value|center:"15" }}`
default	If value evaluates to False, uses the given default. Otherwise, uses the value. For example: `{{ value|default:"nothing" }}`
escape	Escapes a string's HTML.
first	Returns the first item in a list.
join	Joins a list with a string, like Python's `str.join(list)`.
last	Returns the last item in a list.
length	Returns the length of the value. This works for both strings and lists.
linenumbers	Displays text with line numbers.
ljust	Left-aligns the value in a field of a given width.
lower	Converts a string into all lowercase.
random	Returns a random item from the given list.
rjust	Right-aligns the value in a field of a given width.
slice	Returns a slice of the list. Uses the same syntax as Python's list slicing.
time	Formats a time according to the given format.

Table A-5. More Common Built-in Template Filters

Filter	Description
title	Converts a string into title case by making words start with an uppercase character and the remaining characters lowercase
truncatechars	Truncates a string if it is longer than the specified number of characters. Truncated strings will end with a translatable ellipsis sequence (...)
truncatewords	Truncates a string after a certain number of words
upper	Converts a string into all uppercase
urlencode	Escapes a value for use in a URL
wordcount	Returns the number of words

www.ingramcontent.com/pod-product-compliance
Lightning Source LLC
Chambersburg PA
CBHW071414050326
40689CB00010B/1860